The

YES MINISTER

Miscellany

Words by ANTONY JAY & JONATHAN LYNN

Compiled by Iain Dale

biteback ˇˇˇ

First published in Great Britain in 2009 by
Biteback Publishing Ltd
Heal House
375 Kennington Lane
London
SE11 5QY

ISBN 978-1-84954-010-0

A CIP catalogue record for this book is available from the British Library.

Set in Bembo by SoapBox

Printed and bound in Great Britain by TJ International, Padstow

Contents

Introduction

Yes Minister started from two parallel perceptions. The first was
that the television audience was seeing a lot of politics and
politicians but only the bits they were meant to see. There was
a whole world of activity going on behind the scenes that they
were not supposed to know about – the world of Whitehall
where things got done, rather than the world of Westminster
where they were only talked about. The centre of this world
was the minister's private office, and the central figure – the
Permanent Secretary – was someone most of the audience did
not know existed. The tension between him and the minister
was clearly a fruitful source of comedy, with each one needing
the other and yet each having separate and often conflicting
objectives and motivations.

The second perception was that the minister and his Permanent Secretary had an unlikely amount in common with Steptoe & Son. The minister was Young Steptoe, the one who went out and met the public, the one with all the dreams and aspirations, and the Permanent Secretary was Old Steptoe, the one who really understood the business – sceptical, cynical and constantly deflating and frustrating Young Steptoe's plans and projects. Later, we realised that we also owed a great debt to Jeeves and Wooster and to *The Admirable Crichton*: like them, the basic joke of *Yes Minister* was the master who was less able than the servant.

There was a third factor too, which was particularly encouraging. Comedy series can be divided (very roughly) into the domestic and the institutional. We found more comedy potential in institutions – courtrooms, hospitals, army barracks, prisons, hotels – than in living rooms. And in our particular case a series set in Whitehall gave us a sort of insurance policy; if the audience did not find the series particularly funny, they might nevertheless find it sufficiently interesting and informative to be worth switching on again next week. That was a reason, and an important one, why we took a lot of trouble over our research. We talked to a whole lot of people – politicians, political advisors, civil servants – who had worked in ministers' private offices, to make sure that the details were as accurate and authentic as we could make them.

This quest for authenticity produced unexpected benefits. We discovered that truth was not just stranger than fiction, it was also funnier. We often found that if an episode wasn't really working, the answer was to go back to our expert advisors and probe a bit further; time and again this would produce the idea we needed.

There were three plot ideas in particular that we hit on in this way. There was a crisis meeting in the minister's sleeping compartment in the overnight train to the party conference. There was the announcement on television of a Christmas benefit for pensioners after the civil service had refused on the grounds of administrative impossibility, and there was the teetotal reception in an Islamic country where the UK delegation set up an emergency communications tent full of bottles of Scotch to top up the chaste orange juice supplied by their hosts. They all happened, but we would never have thought of them ourselves. But then we would certainly not have thought of a storyline that involved a schizophrenic breaking into Buckingham Palace, walking into the Queen's bedroom and cadging a cigarette. Indeed, if we had submitted such an episode the BBC would probably have rejected it on the grounds of absurdity, and quite right too, until someone did exactly that in July 1982. Truth can be funnier than fiction.

It was a great relief to us to find that the series actually worked. The audience was much bigger than we expected and what was unusual was the Reaction Index, which measures how much the audience enjoyed the programme. For some reason, comedies score lower than, say, documentaries. A successful documentary would score in the seventies, whereas an equally successful comedy would score in the sixties. But *Yes Minister* was in the eighties, and once in the nineties, an area we had thought was the exclusive preserve of David Attenborough and gorillas.

Looking back, it is clear that the first series was the hardest. For one thing, we wrote the first four episodes without knowing who was going to be in it. The BBC kept accepting scripts, paying for them and asking for another without ever fixing a date for a pilot. It was many years before we discovered the reason for this. What happened was that the BBC Head of Comedy, John Howard Davies, was very keen to get Paul Eddington to play Jim Hacker, but Paul was reluctant to commit himself. He was well aware of occasions when actors had signed up for a series on the basis of a single script which they had liked, only to find that it had been written with great care over several months, and once the contract was signed the writer dashed off five more rubbish scripts in a couple of weeks. Both Paul and Nigel Hawthorne liked the first script, but asked for another, and then another, and it wasn't until the delivery of script number four that they felt confident enough to say yes.

Obviously this was not a problem with the second series. We had a cast we knew, but we also had an audience who, during the first series, had come to realise that there was a lot of documentary truth behind the comedy, and that things did really happen like that. Well, sort of. It also made it easier for us when researching stories to explain to people what we were looking for. We have to admit that most of our information came from the political side. Civil servants were extremely discreet and tended not to tell us anything unless they were pretty sure we knew it already or could easily find it out from somewhere else. There was one notable exception. A very distinguished civil servant, Lord Rothschild, invited us to his office and gave us some invaluable insights into the secret world of Whitehall, including an illuminating description of how a Permanent Secretary gets told off – which we later reproduced almost verbatim in a scene where Sir Humphrey is hauled before Sir Arnold, the Cabinet Secretary.

It is interesting, in parenthesis, to note the different reactions of politicians and civil servants to the series. The politicians told us that our representation of politicians was somewhat unconvincing and really rather silly but that we had got the civil servants absolutely right. The civil servants, on the other hand, thought our picture of politicians was spot on, though of course our civil servants bore less relationship to reality. The truth was that we portrayed politicians as civil servants saw them and civil servants as politicians saw them. If we had shown them as they saw themselves, it would have been the most boring programme ever shown on British television.

There was one special problem about the first series. We had put our proposal to the BBC in the summer of 1977, but by the time we had written all the scripts it was late 1978. A pilot was scheduled for January 1979, and after they saw it the BBC decided to go ahead with the series. However, a general election was due to be held by October 1979 at the latest and some people in the BBC were worried that an episode might deal with a sensitive issue in the run-up to the election, so it was finally scheduled for the beginning of 1980. When the Conservatives won, we had a pronoun problem. Was the Prime Minister to be referred to as 'he' or 'she'? If the former, we could be seen as getting at Jim Callaghan; if the latter, Mrs Thatcher. We solved it by never using the personal pronoun. 'The Prime Minister giveth, and the Prime Minister taketh away. Blessed be the name of the Prime Minister.'

Yes Minister and *Yes Prime Minister* ran from 1980 to 1988, but it was never about the 1980s. It was devised in the 1970s and reflected the media-obsessed politics of the Wilson/Heath/Callaghan years, not the conviction politics of Margaret Thatcher. Curiously, it was much closer to the politics of the years after it ended – the years of Major, Blair and Brown.

We had to make Jim Hacker capable of dealing with a wider range of issues than would normally come under a single ministry, so we invented the Department of Administrative Affairs. Even so, after 21 episodes we believed we had dealt with all the most promising areas of conflict between ministers and civil servants, and felt it was time to call it a day. The BBC were very keen for us to go on, but we did not want the programme to become the routine churning out of what were in essence retreads of earlier episodes. Then we had a thought. Suppose Jim became Prime Minister?

All sorts of new possibilities opened up: foreign policy, MI5 and MI6, the nuclear deterrent, spies within government, the armed forces, the American alliance, the appointment of bishops – all subjects we could not include even in the broadest interpretation of the Department of Administrative Affairs.

But how could we credibly make Hacker Prime Minister? Eventually we managed to make him a compromise candidate after removing the present PM and three of his senior colleagues from the running, and produced a one-hour special for Christmas 1984 in which it all happened, followed by two eight-episode series of Yes Prime Minister. Then we really did call it a day.

It was a remarkably happy programme. The three principals – Paul, Nigel and Derek – all liked each other and liked the scripts and their roles, and of course they played them brilliantly. They were so convincing that when Paul visited Australia, the Prime Minister gave him an official welcome at the airport. It certainly had a far wider acceptance than we had ever foreseen; we might have expected some recognition in Commonwealth countries with our form of government, but we certainly didn't expect it to be shown in Libya, Zambia, the Soviet Union or

China, or to be translated into Hindi and performed by an Indian cast. We had, to be honest, thought that its subject matter pretty well restricted it to the UK, but it seems that there is a universal comedy that sparks across the gap between politicians' professions and their actions.

Gogol wrote *The Government Inspector* in the 1830s and it still strikes a chord today. People will always need some sort of government, and those who offer to provide it will not always be motivated solely by a desire to serve their fellows. Between the appearance and the reality, between the intention and the result, between the words and the deeds, there will always be a gap. And as long as that gap is there, political comedy will never die.

Antony Jay
Jonathan Lynn
September 2009

Yes Minister trivia

MINISTRY OF
ADMINISTRATIVE AFFAIRS

FACT FILE

- ♛ The inventors of the series were keen to avoid accusations of party bias. Jim Hacker was placed firmly in the centre of the political spectrum. His headquarters was 'Central House', an amalgam of Conservative Central Office and Labour's Transport House. There were never mentions of political party names and Jim Hacker is depicted with a white rosette at his election count.

- ♛ Yes Minister ran between 1980 and 1984. It lasted for three series, with Yes Prime Minister running from 1986 to 1988 over two series. The first episode of Yes Minister was transmitted on 25 February 1980 on BBC1.

- ♛ There were 38 episodes of the two series. Each lasted for half an hour, apart from 'Party Games' (an hour), in which Jim Hacker became Prime Minister.

♛ Leading cartoonist Gerald Scarfe drew the caricatures of the three main characters which appear in the opening titles.

♛ Not a single scene was set in the House of Commons. Jonathan Lynn comments: 'Government does not take place in the House of Commons; some politics ... and much theatre takes place there. Government happens in private. As in all public performances, the real work is done in rehearsal, behind closed doors. Then the public, and the House, are shown what the government wishes them to see.'

♛ In 2004 a BBC poll ranked Yes Minister sixth in a quest to find Britain's best sitcom.

♛ In 2000 Yes Minister and Yes Prime Minister came joint ninth in the British Film Institute's 100 Greatest Television Programmes list.

♛ Yes Minister won BAFTAs for Best Comedy Series for three years in 1980, 1981 and 1982. Yes Prime Minister was nominated for Best Comedy Series in 1986 and 1987. Antony Jay and Jonathan Lynn won the BAFTA writers' award in 1987.

☖ Nigel Hawthorne won four BAFTAs for Best Light Entertainment Performance in 1981, 1982, 1986 and 1987. Despite being nominated on each occasion, Paul Eddington failed to win.

☖ Several books of the series have been published. The scripts were transformed into prose by Lynn and Jay, and published by BBC Books in the form of diaries. The three series of Yes Minister were published as paperbacks in 1981, 1982 and 1983 respectively before being combined into a revised hardback omnibus edition, The Complete Yes Minister: The Diaries of a Cabinet Minister, in 1984. Two volumes of Yes Prime Minister: The Diaries of the Right Hon. James Hacker were published in 1986 and 1987.

☖ The Complete Yes Minister was on the Sunday Times top ten bestseller list for a total of 106 weeks and was the number 2 bestseller for the decade 1980-1989. Between them, the three volumes were in the top ten bestsellers for more than three years. They have been translated into numerous languages.

♚ Armando Iannucci once compared Yes Minister to George Orwell's 1984 in its influence on the public perception of the role of the state.

♚ The writers consulted Bernard Donoughue and Marcia Falkender, advisors to Harold Wilson and James Callaghan, among many others, on various aspects of the programme.

♚ Famous people who played themselves in the series include psephologist Robert McKenzie, journalist Sue Lawley, newsreader Robert Dougall and broadcaster Ludovic Kennedy.

♚ The theme music was composed by Ronnie Hazlehurst and was based on the chimes of Big Ben. He described it as 'the easiest thing I have ever done'.

♚ In 1997, Derek Fowlds reprised the role of Bernard Woolley to read Antony Jay's How To Beat Sir Humphrey: Every Citizen's Guide to Fighting Officialdom. It was broadcast in three daily parts by Radio 4 from 29 September to 1 October 1997 and released on cassette in October 1997.

- Radio 4 re-recorded sixteen episodes of Yes Minister in two seasons of eight episodes, which were broadcast in the autumns of 1983 and 1984. They were later released on cassette (2000) and on CD (2002).

- When Paul Eddington visited Australia in the 1980s he was treated like a visiting Prime Minister by the then Australian PM Bob Hawke. At a rally, Hawke said: 'You don't want to be listening to me; you want to be listening to the real Prime Minister,' forcing Eddington to improvise a speech.

- The Netherlands, Canada, Sweden, Portugal, Turkey and India have all made their own versions of Yes Minister.

- In the Dutch version, Sir Humphrey was played by a woman and Bernard was played by a Moroccan called Mohammed.

- The Indian version of Yes Minister is called Ji Mantriji and was made in Delhi. References to Russia in the UK version have been changed to Pakistan, cricket becomes football and the references to the EEC have been exchanged for the Commonwealth. Jim

Hacker has been renamed Suryaprakash Singh and is played by the well-known Indian actor Farooq Sheikh. Sir Humphrey is now called Rajnath Mathur and is played by Jayant Kripalani.

👑 Margaret Thatcher was a fan of the show, commenting: 'Its closely observed portrayal of what goes on in the corridors of power has given me hours of pure joy.'

👑 'The Skeleton in the Cupboard' was voted as the best Yes Minister or Yes Prime Minister episode of all time by 1,200 readers of the Yes Minister fan site.

👑 In 1987 a computer game version of Yes Minister was released for the Amstrad CPC, Commodore 64 and ZX Spectrum.

👑 Labour MP Sir Gerald Kaufman described the series as 'The Rt Hon. Faust MP, constantly beset by the wiles of Sir Mephistopheles'.

Sir Humphrey's 'big speeches'

'We love the idea of the coherence and articulacy of Sir Humphrey . . . it's one of the things you look forward to in an episode of Yes Minister . . . when's the big speech going to happen? And can I see if he's reading it from an idiot board . . . he's really learned it, and it's superb.' – *Stephen Fry*

SIR HUMPHREY: I am the Permanent Under Secretary of State, known as the Permanent Secretary. Woolley here is your Principal Private Secretary. I too have a Principal Private Secretary and he is the Principal Private Secretary to the Permanent Secretary. Directly responsible to me are 10 Deputy Secretaries, 87 Under Secretaries and 219 Assistant Secretaries. Directly responsible to the Principal Private Secretary are plain Private Secretaries, and the Prime Minister will be appointing two Parliamentary Under Secretaries and you will be appointing your own Parliamentary Private Secretary.

JIM HACKER: Can they all type?

SIR HUMPHREY: None of us can type, Minister. Mrs McKay types – she's the secretary.

SIR HUMPHREY: Notwithstanding the fact that your proposal could conceivably encompass certain concomitant benefits of a marginal and peripheral relevance, there is a countervailing consideration of infinitely superior magnitude involving your personal complicity and corroborative malfeasance,

with a consequence that the taint and stigma of your
former associations and diversions could irredeemably and
irretrievably invalidate your position and culminate in public
revelations and recriminations of a profoundly embarrassing
and ultimately indefensible character.

JIM HACKER: Perhaps I can have a précis of that?

SIR HUMPHREY: Prime Minister, I must protest in the strongest
possible terms my profound opposition to a newly instituted
practice which imposes severe and intolerable restrictions
upon the ingress and egress of senior members of the
hierarchy and which will, in all probability, should the
current deplorable innovation be perpetuated, precipitate
a constriction of the channels of communication, and
culminate in a condition of organisational atrophy and
administrative paralysis which will render effectively
impossible the coherent and co-ordinated discharge of
the functions of government within Her Majesty's United
Kingdom of Great Britain and Northern Ireland.

JIM HACKER: You mean you've lost your key?

JIM HACKER: People can wait in the lobby or in the state room.

SIR HUMPHREY: Some people. But some people must wait where
other people cannot see the people who are waiting. And people
who arrive before other people must wait where they cannot see
other people who arrive after them being admitted before them.
And people who come in from outside must wait where they
cannot see the people from inside coming in to tell you what
the people from outside are going to see you about. And people

who arrive when you are with people that they are not supposed to know who you have seen must wait somewhere until the people you are not supposed to have seen have seen you.

JIM HACKER: Sounds like an entire Whitehall farce going on.

SIR HUMPHREY: Prime Minister, I have had another word with her. To put it simply, Prime Minister, certain informal discussions took place involving a full and frank exchange of views, after which there arose a series of proposals which on examination proved to indicate certain promising lines of enquiry, which when pursued led to the realisation that the alternative courses of action might in fact, in certain circumstances, be susceptible to discreet modification, leading to a reappraisal of the original areas of difference and pointing a way to encouraging possibilities of compromise and cooperation which if bilaterally implemented with appropriate give and take on both sides might, if the climate were right, have a reasonable possibility at the end of the day of leading rightly or wrongly to a mutually satisfactory resolution.

JIM HACKER: What the hell are you talking about?!

SIR HUMPHREY: We did a deal.

SIR HUMPHREY: And with respect, Prime Minister, I think that the DES will react with some caution to your rather novel proposal.

JIM HACKER: You mean they'll block it?

SIR HUMPHREY: I mean they'll give it the most serious and earnest consideration and insist on a thorough and rigorous examination of all the proposals, allied with detailed feasibility study and budget analysis, before producing a consultative

document for consideration by all interested bodies and
seeking comments and recommendations to be included
in a brief, for a series of working parties who will produce
individual studies which will provide the background for a
more wide-ranging document, considering whether or not
the proposal should be taken forward to the next stage.

JIM HACKER: You mean they'll block it?

SIR HUMPHREY: Yeah.

SIR HUMPHREY: Yes, unfortunately, although the answer was
indeed clear, simple and straightforward, there is some
difficulty in justifiably assigning to it the fourth of the
epithets you applied to the statement, inasmuch as the precise
correlation between the information you communicated
and the facts in so far as they can be determined and
demonstrated is such as to cause epistemological problems
of sufficient magnitude to lay upon the logical and semantic
resources of the English language a heavier burden than they
can reasonably be expected to bear.

JIM HACKER: Epistemological? What are you talking about?

SIR HUMPHREY: You told a lie.

SIR HUMPHREY: If the Prime Minister is told something
personally, even if he doesn't know it officially, he can use his
personal knowledge to start official enquiries to get official
confirmation of personal suspicions so that what he originally
knew personally but not officially he will then know officially
as well as personally.

SIR HUMPHREY: Minister, the traditional allocation of executive responsibilities has always been so determined as to liberate the ministerial incumbent from the administrative minutiae by devolving the managerial functions to those whose experience and qualifications have better formed them for the performance of such humble offices, thereby releasing their political overlords for the more onerous duties and profound deliberations which are the inevitable concomitant of their exalted position.

JIM HACKER: I wonder what made you think I didn't want to hear that?

SIR HUMPHREY: Well, it's clear that the committee has agreed that your new policy is a really excellent plan but in view of some of the doubts being expressed, may I propose that I recall that, after careful consideration, the considered view of the committee was that while they considered that the proposal met with broad approval in principle, that some of the principles were sufficiently fundamental in principle and some of the considerations so complex and finely balanced in practice, that, in principle, it was proposed that the sensible and prudent practice would be to submit the proposal for more detailed consideration, laying stress on the essential continuity of the new proposal with existing principles, and the principle of the principal arguments which the proposal proposes and propounds for their approval, in principle.

Sir Humphrey: It is characteristic of all committee discussions and decisions that every member has a vivid recollection of them, and that every member's recollection of them differs violently from every other member's recollection; consequently we accept the convention that the official decisions are those and only those which have been officially recorded in the minutes by the officials; from which it emerges with elegant inevitability that any decision which has been officially reached would have been officially recorded in the minutes by the officials, and any decision which is not recorded in the minutes by the officials has not been officially reached, even if one or more members believe they can recollect it; so in this particular case, if the decision would have been officially reached, it would have been recorded in the minutes by the officials and it isn't so it wasn't.

Sir Humphrey: Minister, I think there is something you perhaps ought to know.

Jim Hacker: Yes, Humphrey?

Sir Humphrey: The identity of the official whose alleged responsibility for this hypothetical oversight has been the subject of recent discussion is not shrouded in quite such impenetrable obscurity as certain previous disclosures may have led you to assume, but not to put too fine a point on it, the individual in question is, it may surprise you to learn, one whom your present interlocutor is in the habit of defining by means of the perpendicular pronoun.

Jim Hacker: I beg your pardon?
Sir Humphrey: It was . . . I.

Sir Humphrey: Now go in there and inform me of their conversation.
Bernard Woolley: I'm not sure I can do that, Sir Humphrey. It might be confidential.
Sir Humphrey: Bernard, the matter at issue is the defence of the realm and the stability of the government.
Bernard Woolley: But you only need to know things on a need-to-know basis.
Sir Humphrey: I need to know everything! How else can I judge whether or not I need to know it?
Bernard Woolley: So that means you need to know things even when you don't need to know. You need to know them not because you need to know them, but because you need to know whether or not you need to know. And if you don't need to know you still need to know, so that you know there is no need to know.

Sir Humphrey: As far as we can see, looking at it by and large, taking one thing with another, then in the last analysis it is probably true to say, at the end of the day, you would find, in general terms, that, not to put too fine a point on it, there really was not very much in it one way or the other.

Sir Humphrey: It is axiomatic in government that hornets' nests should be left unstirred; cans of worms should remain unopened, cats should not be set among the pigeons. Ministers should also leave boats unrocked, nettles ungrasped, refrain from taking bulls by the horns, and resolutely turn their backs to the music.

SIR HUMPHREY: If there had been investigations, which there haven't, or not necessarily, or I'm not at liberty to say whether there have, there would have been a project team which, had it existed, on which I cannot comment, would now have disbanded, if it had existed, and the members returned to their original departments, if indeed there had been any such members.

SIR HUMPHREY: The Special Branch has reason to believe that the threat to your life has been diminished.

JIM HACKER: How do they know?

SIR HUMPHREY: Surveillance. They overheard a conversation.

JIM HACKER: What did it say?

SIR HUMPHREY: Oh, I don't think it is of any—

JIM HACKER: Come on, Humphrey, I have a right to know!

SIR HUMPHREY: Well, it was a conversation to the effect that, in view of the somewhat nebulous and inexplicit nature of your remit, and the arguably marginal and peripheral nature of your influence on the central deliberations and decisions within the political process, there could be a case for restructuring their action priorities in such a way as to eliminate your liquidation from their immediate agenda.

JIM HACKER: They said that??

SIR HUMPHREY: That was the gist of it.

SIR HUMPHREY: There are certain items of confidential information which, while in theory they might be susceptible to innocent interpretation, do nevertheless contain a certain element of, shall we say, ambiguity, so that were they to be presented in a less than generous manner or to an uncharitable mind, they might be a source of considerable embarrassment, even conceivably hazard, were they to impinge on the deliberations of an office of more than usual sensitivity.

JIM HACKER: I'm sorry?

CHIEF WHIP: He's talking about security questions.

SIR HUMPHREY: Questions of administrative policy can cause confusion between the administration of a policy and the policy of administration, especially when responsibility for the administration conflicts or overlaps with responsibility for the policy of the administration of the policy.

Bernard's pedantry

JIM HACKER: Now, about nailing that leak—

BERNARD WOOLLEY: I'm sorry to be pedantic, but if you nail a leak you make another.

BERNARD WOOLLEY: Apparently, the fact that you needed to know was not known at the time that the now-known need to know was known, therefore those that needed to advise and inform the Home Secretary perhaps felt the information he needed as to whether to inform the highest authority of the known information was not yet known and therefore there was no authority for the authority to be informed because the need to know was not, at that time, known or needed.

BERNARD WOOLLEY: May I just clarify this? You think the National Theatre thinks that you are bluffing and the National Theatre thinks that you think that they are bluffing, whereas your bluff is to make the National Theatre think that you are bluffing when you are not bluffing, or if you are bluffing, your bluff is to make them think you are not bluffing. And their bluff must be that they're bluffing, because if they're not bluffing they're not bluffing.

Bernard's ideas for slogans to make the department more popular:

1. Administration saves the nation!
2. Red tape is fun!
3. Red tape holds the nation together!

JIM HACKER: Bernard, this government is here to govern, not merely preside like our predecessors did. When a country is going downhill, it is time for someone to get into the driving seat and put his foot on the accelerator.

BERNARD WOOLLEY: I think you mean the brake.

SIR HUMPHREY: The head of state must greet a head of state even if he's not here as the head of state.

BERNARD WOOLLEY: It's all a matter of hats, Minister.

JIM HACKER: Hats?

BERNARD WOOLLEY: Yes. You see, he is coming here wearing his head-of-government hat; he is the head of state too, but it's not a state visit because he's not wearing his head-of-state hat. Protocol demands that even though he's wearing his head-of-government hat, he must still be met by the crown.

JIM HACKER: Fortunately, Bernard, most of our journalists are so incompetent that they have the gravest difficulty in finding out that today is Wednesday.

BERNARD WOOLLEY: It's actually Thursday, Minister.

JIM HACKER: But we can't stab our partners in the back and spit in their face.

BERNARD WOOLLEY: You can't stab anyone in the back while you spit in their face.

JIM HACKER: Bernard, how did Sir Humphrey know I was with Dr Cartwright?

BERNARD WOOLLEY: God moves in a mysterious way.

JIM HACKER: Let me make one thing perfectly clear: Humphrey is not God, okay?

BERNARD WOOLLEY: Will you tell him or shall I?

JIM HACKER: Tell me how he knew where I was.

BERNARD WOOLLEY: Well, confidentially, Minister, everything you tell me is in complete confidence, so equally, and I am sure you appreciate this, and by 'appreciate' I don't actually mean appreciate, I mean understand, that everything Sir Humphrey tells me is also in complete confidence, as indeed everything I tell you is in complete confidence, and for that matter everything I tell Sir Humphrey is in complete confidence.

JIM HACKER: So?

BERNARD WOOLLEY: So in complete confidence, I am confident that you understand that for me to keep Sir Humphrey's confidence and your confidence means that conversations between him and me must be completely confidential, as confidential in fact as conversations between you and me are completely confidential.

JIM HACKER: So they insult me and then expect me to give them more money?

SIR HUMPHREY: Yes, I must say it's a rather undignified posture. But it is what artists always do: crawling towards the government on their knees, shaking their fists.

JIM HACKER: Beating me over the head with their begging bowls.

BERNARD WOOLLEY: Oh, I'm sorry to be pedantic, Prime Minister, but they can't beat you over the head if they're on their knees. Unless of course they've got very long arms.

The Thatcher script

In January 1984 Margaret Thatcher performed a sketch with
Jim and Sir Humphrey at an awards ceremony hosted by
Mary Whitehouse's National Viewers & Listeners Association.
At the time it was thought that Mrs Thatcher had written it
herself, but it emerged later that her Press Secretary, Bernard
Ingham, had composed most of it. Nigel Hawthorne and Paul
Eddington, who were not political supporters of the Iron Lady,
were very unenthusiastic at the prospect of appearing alongside
her. Margaret Thatcher, although not known for having a great
sense of humour, was a big fan of the programme. Accepting
the award from the NVLA, writer Jonathan Lynn thanked Mrs
Thatcher 'for taking her rightful place in the field of situation
comedy'. Everyone laughed, except the Prime Minister.

PRIME MINISTER: Ah, good morning Jim, Sir Humphrey. Do come in and sit down. How's your wife? Is she well?

JIM HACKER: *[puzzled]* Oh yes, fine, Prime Minister. Fine. Thank you. Yes, fine.

PRIME MINISTER: Good. So pleased. I've been meaning to have a word with you for some time. I've got an idea.

JIM HACKER: *[brightening visibly]* An idea, Prime Minister? Oh good.

SIR HUMPHREY: *[guardedly]* An idea, Prime Minister?

PRIME MINISTER: Well, not really an idea. It's gone beyond that, actually. I've given it quite a bit of thought and I'm sure you, Jim, are the right man to carry it out. It's got to do with a kind of institution and you are sort of responsible for institutions, aren't you?

SIR HUMPHREY: *[cautiously]* Institutions, Prime Minister?

JIM HACKER: *[decisively]* Oh yes, institutions fall to me. Most definitely. And you want me to set one up, I suppose?

PRIME MINISTER: Set one up? Certainly not. I want you to get rid of one.

JIM HACKER: *[astonished]* Get rid of one, Prime Minister?

PRIME MINISTER: Yes. It's all very simple. I want you to abolish economists.

JIM HACKER: *[mouth open]* Abolish economists, Prime Minister?

PRIME MINISTER: Yes, abolish economists . . . quickly.

SIR HUMPHREY: *[silkily]* *All* of them, Prime Minister?

PRIME MINISTER: Yes, all of them. They never agree on anything. They just fill the heads of politicians with all sorts of curious notions, like the more you spend, the richer you get.

JIM HACKER: *[coming around to the idea]* I see your point, Prime

Minister. Can't have the nation's time wasted on curious notions, can we? No.

Sir Humphrey: *[sternly]* Minister.

Prime Minister: Quite right, Jim. Absolute waste of time. Simply got to go.

Jim Hacker: *[uncertain]* Simply got to go?

Prime Minister: *[motherly]* Yes, Jim. Don't worry. If it all goes wrong I shall get the blame. But if it goes right – as it will – then you'll get the credit for redeploying a lot of underused and misapplied resources. Probably get promotion too.

Sir Humphrey: *[indignantly]* Resources? Resources, Prime Minister? We're talking about economists.

Prime Minister: 'Were', Sir Humphrey. 'Were'.

Jim Hacker: *[decisively]* Yes, Humphrey, 'were'. We're going to get rid of them.

PRIME MINISTER: Well, it's all settled then. I look forward to receiving your plan for abolition soon. Tomorrow, shall we say? I'd like you to announce it before it all leaks.

JIM HACKER: *[brightly]* Tomorrow then, Prime Minister.

PRIME MINISTER: Yes. Well, go and sort it out. Now, Sir Humphrey . . . what did you say your degree was?

SIR HUMPHREY: *[innocently]* Degree, Prime Minister?

PRIME MINISTER: *[firmly]* Yes, Sir Humphrey, degree. Your degree. You have one, I take it – most Permanent Secretaries do – or perhaps two?

SIR HUMPHREY: *[modestly]* Er, well, actually, Prime Minister, a double first.

PRIME MINISTER: Congratulations, Sir Humphrey, but what in?

SIR HUMPHREY: *[weakly]* Politics . . . er . . . and, er . . . economics.

PRIME MINISTER: *[soothingly]* Capital, my dear Sir Humphrey. You'll know exactly where to start.

PRIME MINISTER: *[bleakly]* Yes, Prime Minister.

Exit Jim Hacker and Sir Humphrey

How to be a civil servant

Reorganising the Civil Service is like drawing a knife through a bowl of marbles.

....

JIM HACKER *[to Sir Humphrey]*: In private industry if you screw things up you get the boot; in the civil service if you screw things up *I* get the boot.

....

A Private Secretary should not have to decide whether he's on the minister's side or the department's side when the chips are down. His job is to see the chips stay up.

....

You cannot call Civil Service delays 'tactics'. That would be to mistake lethargy for strategy.

....

The opposition are not the real opposition. They are the government in exile. The Civil Service is the opposition in residence.

....

Opposition's about asking awkward questions. And government is about not answering them.

....

He who drafts the document wins the day.

....

[How to deal with a nonsensical complaint]

BERNARD WOOLLEY: We can CGSM it.

JIM HACKER: CGSM?

BERNARD: Civil Service code, Minister. It stands for 'Consignment of Geriatric Shoe Manufacturers'.

JIM: What?

BERNARD: A load of old cobblers, Minister.

JIM: I'm not a civil servant; I shall use my own code. I shall write 'Round objects'.

....

If a matter is *under consideration* it means we've lost the file. *Under active consideration* means we're trying to find it.

....

JIM HACKER: Twenty-three thousand. In the Department of Administrative Affairs. Twenty-three thousand people just for administering other administrators. We have to do a time-and-motion study, see who we can get rid of.

SIR HUMPHREY: We did one of those last year.

JIM: And?

HUMPHREY: It transpired that we needed another 500 people.

....

The public do not know anything about wasting public money. We are the experts.

....

We are here to see that the Prime Minister is not confused. Politicians are simple people. They like simple choices. Clear guidance. They don't like doubt and conflict.

The Civil Service merely exists to implement legislation that is enacted by Parliament. So long as Parliament continues to legislate for more and more control over people's lives, the Civil Service must grow.

Civil servants should not discuss moral issues with politicians. It is a serious misuse of government time.

A Civil Service computer strike would bring government to a standstill if it were not for the fact that it is already.

If you do not want Cabinet to spend too long discussing something, make it last on the agenda before lunch.

The Civil Service, when drafting a minister's speech, is primarily concerned with making him nail his trousers to the mast. Then he can't climb down!

A cover-up is merely a responsible decision exercised in the national interest to prevent unnecessary disclosure of eminently justifiable procedures in which untimely revelation would severely impair public confidence.

Once you allow ministers to write draft reports, the next thing you know they'll be drafting government policy.

To block civil servants' honours until they had achieved economies would create a very dangerous precedent.

Since Cabinet ministers are incapable of understanding a paper more than three pages long, we put a one-page summary on the front. The Janet and John bit.

It is important to put political advisors in rooms as far away as possible from the Prime Minister. Influence diminishes with distance.

If civil servants could remove politicians on grounds of incompetence it would empty the House of Commons, remove the Cabinet, be the end of democracy and the beginning of responsible government.

Ministers are ignorant not because we do not give them the right answers but because they do not ask us the right questions.

If we cannot refute the arguments in a paper, we simply discredit the person who wrote it. This is called playing the man and not the ball.

In the great restaurant of government civil servants are the cooks and politicians are the waiters. We prepare all the dishes, and they serve them up to the customers.

A minister's private office can be kept busy without actually doing anything but producing drafts – drafts for statements he doesn't make, speeches he doesn't deliver, press releases nobody prints, papers nobody reads, and answers to questions nobody asks him.

We do not have to accept a political advisor just because the PM likes her. Samson liked Delilah.

The civil service is neither right wing nor left wing. Political bias varies from department to department. Defence, whose clients are military, is right wing whereas Health, dealing with health unions and social workers, is left wing. Industry, dealing with employers, is right wing; Employment, dealing with unions, is left wing. The Home Office – police, prison warders, immigration officers – is right wing. Education – teachers and lecturers – is left wing. The result is a perfectly balanced and neutral civil service.

Civil servants need great flexibility. They have to be constantly prepared to change horses in mid-stream as politicians change what they are pleased to call their minds.

The job of a professionally conducted internal enquiry is to unearth a great mass of no evidence.

Too much civil service work consists of circulating information that isn't relevant about subjects that don't matter to people who aren't interested.

It is our job to tell select committees the truth and nothing but the truth. But it would be profoundly inappropriate and grossly irresponsible to tell them the whole truth.

Once you specify in advance what a government project
is going to cost, what it is supposed to achieve, and whose
job it is to see that it does, the entire system of civil service
administration collapses and you are into the whole squalid
world of professional management.

The secret of success in the Civil Service is to secure extra
budget staff and premises by taking on a difficult job, then
quietly change the remit so that all the difficult bits are either
removed or made the responsibility of other people.

Any unwelcome initiative by a minister can be delayed until
after the next election by the Civil Service twelve-stage
delaying procedure:

1.   Informal discussions
2.   Draft proposal
3.   Preliminary study
4.   Discussion document
5.   In-depth study
6.   Revised proposal
7.   Policy statement
8.   Strategy statement
9.   Discussion of strategy
10. Implementation plan circulated
11. Revised implementation plans
12. Cabinet agreement.

Moving civil servants to a new job every three years is a great insurance against failure. Since most major projects take more than three years, the man in charge at the end can say it failed because it was started wrong and the man in charge at the beginning can say it failed because it was finished wrong. In the unlikely event of it succeeding they can both take the credit.

Conjurors offer the audience any card in the pack and always get them to take the one they want. This is the way we in the Civil Service get ministers to take decisions.

If civil servants did not fight for the budgets of their departments, they could end up with departments so small that even ministers could run them.

A government economy drive means three days of press releases, three weeks of ministerial memos, then a crisis in the Middle East and back to normal again.

Giving powers of decision to the Civil Service helps to take government out of politics. That is Britain's only hope of survival.

Three varieties of Civil Service silence:

1. Discreet silence: the silence when we do not want to tell them the facts.
2. Stubborn silence: the silence when we do not intend to take any action.
3. Courageous silence: the silence when they catch us out and we haven't got a leg to stand on. Then one should imply that we could vindicate ourselves completely if only we were free to tell all, but we are too honourable to do so.

When a problem is too difficult ministers set up Royal Commissions and civil servants set up inter-departmental committees. This bequeaths it to the next generation.

We dare not allow politicians to establish the principle that senior civil servants can be removed for incompetence. We could lose dozens of our chaps. Hundreds maybe. Even thousands.

JUMBO: We should never let ministers get so deeply involved. Once they start writing the draft, the next thing we know they'll be dictating policy.

It is axiomatic with civil servants that information should only be repeated to their political 'masters' when absolutely necessary, and to the public when absolutely unavoidable.

Civil servants are grown like oak trees, not mustard and cress. They bloom and ripen with the seasons. They mature like an old port.

Any document that removes the power of decision from ministers and gives it to the Civil Service is important.

The Civil Service generally hopes there'll be no movement on any subject.

When things go wrong, a minister's first instinct is to rat on his department. A civil servant's first instinct is to rat on another department.

The ordinary rules of living don't apply to civil servants: they don't suffer from unemployment, they automatically get honours, and inflation simply increases their pensions.

The three articles of Civil Service faith:
1. It takes longer to do things quickly.
2. It's more expensive to do things cheaply.
3. It's more democratic to do things secretly.

The humility of Sir Humphrey Appleby

I am neither pro or anti anything. I am merely a humble vessel into which ministers pour the fruits of their deliberations.

AGNES MOORHOUSE: Animals have rights too, you know. A battery chicken's life isn't worth living. Would you want to spend your life packed in with 600 other desperate, squawking, smelly creatures, unable to breathe fresh air, unable to move, unable to stretch, unable to think?

SIR HUMPHREY: Certainly not; that is why I never stood for Parliament.

Translating
Civil Service speak

'Special Development Areas.'
Translation: Marginal constituencies.

'Assistance to areas of economic hardship.'
Translation: Pouring money into marginal constituencies.

'Decentralisation of government.'
Translation: Moving government offices into marginal consistencies.

'Sometimes one is forced to consider the possibility that affairs are being conducted in a manner which, all things being considered and making all possible allowances, is, not to put too fine a point on it, perhaps not entirely straightforward.'
Translation: You're lying.

'This is an urgent problem and we therefore propose setting up a Royal Commission.'
Translation: The problem is a bloody nuisance, but we hope that by the time a Royal Commission reports, four years from now, everyone will have forgotten about it or we can find someone else to blame.

'**A phased reduction of about 100,000 people is not in the public interest.**'
Translation: It is in the public interest but it is not in the interest of the Civil Service.

'**Ministers have an enviable intellectual suppleness and moral manoeuvrability.**'
Translation: You can't trust them further than you can throw them.

'**Somewhat unorthodox procedure.**'
Translation: The act of a gibbering lunatic.

'**I think we are going to have to be very careful.**'
Translation: We are not going to do this.

'**Have you thought through all the implications?**'
Translation: You are not going to do this.

'**It is a slightly puzzling decision.**'
Translation: Minister, that is the silliest thing I have ever heard.

'Public opinion is not yet ready for such a step.'
Translation: Public opinion is ready but the Civil Service is not.

'The police have suffered an acute personnel establishment shortfall.'
Translation: Short staffed.

'We have decided to be more flexible in our application of this principle.'
Translation: We are dropping this policy but we don't want to admit it publicly.

'House training.'
Translation: Making a new Prime Minister see things our way.

Like a sieve

I don't want a leak enquiry, I want to find out who did it.

Leak enquiries are for setting up, not for conducting.

One of the Cabinet has been leaking to the press. In one week he has been an unofficial spokesman and informed source, a senior colleague of the PM, a source close to the leadership, and a growing body of opinion within the party.

To suppress an internal government report, rewrite it as official advice to the minister. As it is against the rules to publish it, you can leak the bits you have rewritten to friendly journalists.

Politicians are more leaked against than leaking.

It's too dangerous to publish the results of an enquiry because most leaks come from Number 10. The ship of state is the only vessel that leaks from the top.

First Law of Political Indiscretion: Always have a drink before you leak.

How to discredit a report

Stage one: Refuse to publish in the public interest, saying:
1. There are security considerations
2. The findings could be misinterpreted
3. You are waiting for the results of a wider and more detailed report, which is still in preparation. (If there isn't one, commission it; this gives you even more time.)

Stage two: Discredit the evidence you are not publishing because:
1. It leaves important questions unanswered
2. Much of the evidence is inconclusive
3. The figures are open to other interpretations
4. Certain findings are contradictory
5. Some of the main conclusions have been questioned. (If they haven't, question them yourself; then they have.)

Stage three: Undermine the recommendations. Suggested phrases:
1. 'Not really a basis for long-term decisions'
2. 'Not sufficient information on which to base a valid assessment'
3. 'No reason for any fundamental rethink of existing policy'
4. 'Broadly speaking, it endorses current practice'.

Stage four: Discredit the person who produced the report. Explain (off the record) that:
1. He is harbouring a grudge against the department
2. He is a publicity seeker
3. He is trying to get a knighthood/chair/vice-chancellorship
4. He wants to be a consultant to a multinational.

How to stall a minister

1. The administration is in its early months and there's an awful lot to do at once.
2. Something ought to be done but is this the right way to achieve it?
3. The idea is good but the time is not ripe.
4. The proposal has run into technical, logistic and legal difficulties which are being sorted out.
5. Never refer to the matter or reply to the minister's notes. By the time he or she taxes you with it face to face you should be able to say it looks unlikely if anything can be done until after the election.
6. To drop the whole scheme, recommend: (1) a pause to regroup, (2) a lull in which we reassess the position and discuss alternative strategies and (3) a space for time for mature reflection and deliberation.

Delaying phrases:
1. The subject is still under discussion.
2. The programme is not yet finalised.
3. Nothing precipitate should be done.
4. Failing instructions to the contrary, I propose that we await developments.

A foreign affair

The Foreign Office never expects the Cabinet to agree to any of their policies. That's why they never fully explain them.

The Foreign Office is pro-Europe because it is really anti-Europe. The Civil Service was united in its desire to make sure the Common Market didn't work. That's why we went into it.

The Foreign Office aren't there to do things. They're there to explain why things can't be done.

Standard Foreign Office four-stage response to any crisis:
1. Say nothing is going to happen.
2. Say something may be going to happen, but we should do nothing about it.
3. Say maybe we should do something about it, but there's nothing we *can* do.
4. Say maybe there was something we could have done but it's too late now.

In Arab countries women get stoned when they commit adultery. In Britain they commit adultery when they get stoned.

Britain should always be on the side of law and justice, so long as we don't allow it to affect our foreign policy.

Issuing a statement

The usual six options are:
1.   Do nothing.
2.   Issue a statement deploring the speech.
3.   Lodge an official protest.
4.   Cut off aid.
5.   Break off diplomatic relations.
6.   Declare war.

Problems:
1.   If we do nothing we implicitly agree with the speech.
2.   If we issue a statement we'll just look foolish.
3.   If we lodge a protest it'll be ignored.
4.   We can't cut off aid because we don't give them any.
5.   If we break off diplomatic relations we can't negotiate the oil rig contracts.
6.   If we declare war it might just look as though we were over-reacting.

It was a good idea to partition countries like India, Cyprus, Palestine and Ireland as a part of their independence. It keeps them busy fighting each other so that we don't have to have a policy about them.

SIR HUMPHREY: There is the excuse we used for the Munich Agreement: It occurred before certain important facts were known, and couldn't happen again.

JIM HACKER: What important facts?

SIR HUMPHREY: Well, that Hitler wanted to conquer Europe.

JIM HACKER: I thought that everybody knew that.

SIR HUMPHREY: Not the Foreign Office.

JIM HACKER: Apparently, the White House thinks that the Foreign Office is full of pinkoes and traitors.

BERNARD WOOLLEY: No, it's not. Well, not full.

Giving information to Moscow is serious. Giving information to anyone is serious. Some information would do Britain less harm if given to the Kremlin than if given to the Cabinet.

As far as world politics goes, the Foreign Office is just an irrelevance. We have no real power, we are just a sort of American missile base.

Foreign Office Honours:
CMG: 'Call Me God'
KCMG: 'Kindly Call Me God'
GCMG: 'God Calls Me God'.

People have said a lot of unpleasant things about the Foreign Office, but no one has ever accused them of patriotism.

The Foreign Office are not spineless. It takes a great deal of strength to do nothing all the time.

It is well known that in the Foreign Office an order from the Prime Minister becomes a request from the Foreign Secretary, then a recommendation from the minister of state, finally just a suggestion from the ambassador. If it ever gets that far.

Foreign policy must be made in the Foreign Office. It cannot be left to yobbos like Fleet Street editors, backbench MPs and Cabinet ministers.

The term 'underdeveloped countries' was considered offensive. So they called them 'developing countries'. This term apparently was patronising. Then they became 'less developed countries', or LDCs for short. The term 'less developed countries' is not yet causing offence to anyone. When it does, we are to immediately replace the term LDCs with HRRCs. This is short for 'human resource-rich countries'. In other words, they are grossly overpopulated and begging for money.

The Foreign Office is a hotbed of cold feet.

The letters JB in capitals are one of the highest Commonwealth honours. They stand for 'Jailed by the British'. The order includes Gandhi, Nkrumah, Makarios, Ben Gurion, Kenyatta, Nehru and many other world leaders.

JIM HACKER: Humphrey, who is it who has the last word about the government of Britain? The British Cabinet or the American President?

SIR HUMPHREY: You know, that is a fascinating question. We often discuss it.

JIM HACKER: And what conclusion have you arrived at?

SIR HUMPHREY: Well, I must admit to be a bit of a heretic. I think it is the British Cabinet. But I know I am in the minority.

Diplomatic manoeuvres

BERNARD WOOLLEY: No, we can't have alphabetical seating in the Abbey: you would have Iraq and Iran next to each other. Plus Israel and Jordan, all sitting in the same pew. We would be in danger of starting World War III.

One Prime Minister's lunch with an ambassador destroys two years of patient diplomacy.

The English-speaking nations can be said, with a certain generosity of spirit, to include the United States.

You can't put a nation's interest at risk just because of some silly sentimentality about justice.

The United Nations is the accepted forum for the expression of international hatred.

Our European 'partners'

Britain has had the same foreign policy objective for at least
the last 500 years: to create a disunited Europe. In that cause
we have fought with the Dutch against the Spanish, with the
Germans against the French, with the French and Italians against
the Germans, and with the French against the Germans and
Italians. Divide and rule, you see. Why should we change now
when it's worked so well?

Current policy: to break the whole thing [the EEC] up. So
we had to get inside. We tried to break it up from the outside,
but that wouldn't work. Now that we're inside we can make a
complete pig's breakfast of the whole thing: set the Germans
against the French, the French against the Italians, the Italians
against the Dutch. The Foreign Office is terribly pleased, it's just
like old times.

The EU is just like the United Nations. The more members it
has, the more arguments you can stir up, and the more futile and
impotent it becomes.

A NATO award given once every five years: a gold medal,
a big ceremony in Brussels, and £100,000 for the statesman
who's made the biggest contribution to European unity since
Napoleon. If you don't count Hitler.

The typical Common Market official has the organising capacity of the Italians, the flexibility of the Germans, the modesty of the French, the imagination of the Belgians, the generosity of the Dutch and intelligence of the Irish.

What will the Greeks want out of the EEC? An olive mountain and a retsina lake.

Brussels is full of hard-working public servants who have to endure a lot of exhausting travel and tedious entertainment.

We sometimes get our own way with the French. The last time was the Battle of Waterloo, 1815.

Europe is a not a community of nations, dedicated towards one goal. It's a game played for national interests, it always was. We did not go into it to strengthen the brotherhood of free Western nations, we went in to screw the French by splitting them off from the Germans. The French went into it to protect their inefficient farmers from commercial competition. The Germans went in to cleanse themselves of genocide and apply for readmission to the human race. Luxembourg is in it for the perks; the capital of the EEC, all that foreign money pouring in. With the administration in Brussels and the parliament in Strasbourg, it's like having the House of Commons in Swindon and the Civil Service in Kettering.

Excuses, excuses

The Comprehensive School Excuse: it's only gone wrong because of heavy cuts in staff and budgets which have stretched supervisory resources beyond the limit.

The Charge of the Light Brigade Excuse: it was an unfortunate lapse by an individual which has been dealt with under internal disciplinary procedures.

The Munich Agreement Excuse: it occurred before important facts were known, and cannot happen again.

The Anthony Blunt Excuse: there is a perfectly satisfactory explanation for everything, but security prevents its disclosure.

The Concorde Excuse: it was a worthwhile experiment now abandoned but not before it provided much valuable data and considerable employment.

We don't do God

It is interesting that nowadays politicians want to talk about morals and bishops want to talk about politics.

An atheist clergyman couldn't continue to draw his stipend. So when they stop believing in God they call themselves modernists.

The Church is looking for a candidate to maintain the balance – between those who believe in God and those that don't.

Nowadays, bishops only wear gaiters at significant religious events like the royal garden party.

The Queen is inseparable from the Church of England. God is what is called an optional extra.

Bishops tend to have long lives – apparently the Lord isn't all that keen for them to join him.

The plans for a new church in South London had places for dispensing orange juice, family planning and organising demos, but nowhere to celebrate Holy Communion.

Theology is a device for helping agnostics to stay within the Church of England.

Getting the PM to choose the right bishop is like a conjuror getting a member of the audience to choose a card. With the Church of England, the choice is usually between a knave and a queen.

Bishops need to be someone to look up to: the sort of chaps who speak properly and know which knife and fork to use.

Dear Ladies

If you go around promoting women just because they are the best person for the job, you could cause a lot of resentment throughout the Civil Service. We must always have the right to promote the best man for the job, regardless of sex.

JIM HACKER: What happens when a minister is a woman, what'll you call her?

SIR HUMPHREY: Yes, that is rather interesting. We sought an answer to that point when I was Principal Private Secretary and Dr Edith Summerskill – as she then was – was appointed minister in 1947. I didn't quite like to refer to her as my mistress.

JIM HACKER: What was the answer?

SIR HUMPHREY: Oh, we're still waiting for it.

If we are to have a 25 per cent quota of women, we must have a much larger intake at the recruitment stage. So that eventually we'll have 25 per cent in the top jobs – in 25 years.

JIM HACKER: I have made a policy decision. I am going to do something about the number of women in the Civil Service.

SIR HUMPHREY: Surely there aren't all that many?

Blessed be the Prime Minister

SIR HUMPHREY: Bernard, what would you say to your present
    master as the next Prime Minister?
BERNARD WOOLLEY: The Minister?
SIR HUMPHREY: Yes.
BERNARD: Mr Hacker?
SIR HUMPHREY: Yes.
BERNARD: As Prime Minister?
SIR HUMPHREY: Yes.
[Bernard checks his watch.]
SIR HUMPHREY: Are you in a hurry?
BERNARD: No, I'm just checking to see it wasn't April the first.

If asked if he wants to be Prime Minister, the generally
acceptable answer for a politician is that while he does not seek
the office, he was pleased to offer himself to the service of his
country, and that should his colleagues persuade him that that is
the best way he can serve, he might reluctantly have to accept
the responsibility, whatever his personal wishes might be.

Prime Ministers cannot be stopped but they can be slowed
down until a few crises have absorbed their reforming zeal.

Things don't happen just because Prime Ministers are keen on
them. Neville Chamberlain was keen on peace.

Prime Ministers have had no proper selection of training, so it is our patriotic duty to arrange for them to make the right decisions as often as possible.

JIM HACKER: It's the people's will. I am their leader; I must follow them.

If the Prime Minister talks to underlings he may learn things that we don't know. Our whole position could be undermined.

SIR HUMPHREY: Hello, Bernard, I hear the Prime Minister wants to see me?
BERNARD WOOLLEY: Yes, Sir Humphrey.
SIR HUMPHREY: What's his problem?
BERNARD WOOLLEY: Education.
SIR HUMPHREY: Well, it's a bit late to do anything about that now.

The Prime Minister never thinks it is silly to appoint people who are vain and incompetent. Look at the Cabinet.

It is my job to protect the Prime Minister from the great tide of irrelevant information that beats against the walls of 10 Downing Street every day.

The Prime Minister doesn't want the truth – he wants something he can tell Parliament.

Most Prime Ministers have run out of steam by the end of their first year and ground to a halt by the end of the second. Then you can steer them into the world statesman role and your troubles are over.

The Prime Minister gets his own car and driver, free air travel, a nice flat in central London, a house in the country, endless publicity, lots of banquets, a decent salary and a pension for life. It is unpardonable greed if he also wants to take over from the Civil Service the job of running the country.

Defence of the realm

Conventional forces are terribly expensive. Much cheaper just to press a button.

SIR HUMPHREY: With Trident we could obliterate the whole of eastern Europe.

JIM HACKER: I don't want to obliterate the whole of eastern Europe.

SIR HUMPHREY: It's a deterrent.

JIM HACKER: It's a bluff. I probably wouldn't use it.

SIR HUMPHREY: Yes, but they don't know that you probably wouldn't.

JIM HACKER: They probably do.

SIR HUMPHREY: Yes, they probably know that you probably wouldn't. But they can't certainly know.

JIM HACKER: They probably certainly know that I probably wouldn't.

SIR HUMPHREY: Yes, but even though they probably certainly know that you probably wouldn't, they don't certainly know that, although you probably wouldn't, there is no probability that you certainly would.

JIM HACKER: Maths has become politicised: 'If it costs £5 billion a year to maintain Britain's nuclear defences and £75 a year to feed a starving African child, how many African children can be saved from starvation if the Ministry of Defence abandons nuclear weapons?'

SIR HUMPHREY: That's easy: none. They'd spend it all on conventional weapons. The Cabinet must not be allowed to talk too much about defence policy, or they will end up thinking about it. Then we shall be in trouble.

SIR HUMPHREY: Don't you believe that Great Britain should have the best?

JIM HACKER: Yes, of course.

SIR HUMPHREY: Very well, if you walked into a nuclear missile showroom you would buy Trident – it's lovely, it's elegant, it's beautiful. It is quite simply the best. And Britain should have the best. In the world of the nuclear missile it is the Savile Row suit, the Rolls-Royce Corniche, the Château Lafite 1945. It is the nuclear missile Harrods would sell you. What more can I say?

JIM HACKER: Only that it costs £15 billion and we don't need it.

SIR HUMPHREY: Well, you can say that about anything at Harrods.

SIR HUMPHREY: Bernard, what is the purpose of our defence policy?

BERNARD WOOLLEY: To defend Britain.

SIR HUMPHREY: No, Bernard. It is to make people believe Britain is defended.

BERNARD WOOLLEY: The Russians?

SIR HUMPHREY: Not the Russians, the British! The Russians know it is not.

JIM HACKER: We should always fight for the weak against the strong.

SIR HUMPHREY: Well, why don't we send troops to Afghanistan to fight the Russians?

JIM HACKER: The Russians are too strong.

JIM HACKER: Oh, this is nice. The Americans are delighted by our little goodwill visit to St George's Island. That's good, isn't it?

SIR HUMPHREY: Excellent...

JIM HACKER: They say they have got a whole airborne division ready if we want reinforcements.

SIR HUMPHREY: Reinforcements of what?

JIM HACKER: Reinforcements of goodwill, Humphrey!

The problem of the Ministry of Defence is that in peacetime the three armed forces have no one on whom to vent their warlike instincts except the Cabinet or each other.

JIM HACKER: Tell me, General, where is the Hot Line?

GENERAL HOWARD: Which one?

JIM HACKER: The one to Russia.

BERNARD WOOLLEY: The Red Hot Line, Sir.

GENERAL HOWARD: That's in Downing Street.

JIM HACKER: So in an emergency, I can get straight through to the Soviet President?

GENERAL HOWARD: Theoretically, yes.

JIM HACKER: Theoretically?

GENERAL HOWARD: That's what we tell journalists. In fact, we did once get through to the Kremlin, but only to a switchboard operator.

JIM HACKER: Couldn't the operator put you through?

GENERAL HOWARD: We never found out. He didn't seem to speak much English.

BERNARD WOOLLEY: That is why that torpedo landed on Sandwich golf course.

JIM HACKER: Sandwich golf course? I didn't read that in the paper.

BERNARD WOOLLEY: No, of course not: there was a cover-up. The members just found a new bunker on the seventh fairway the next day.

The army, a small, tough, elite force, resists conscription because it is terrified of finding itself guarding a mob of punks, freaks, riff-raff, junkies and football hooligans with nothing to do except peel potatoes in Aldershot.

Shuffling the pack

JIM HACKER: Where will I go?

SIR HUMPHREY: Er, well, there is a rumour, Minister.

JIM HACKER: Rumour? What rumour?

SIR HUMPHREY: Minister with General Responsibility for Industrial Harmony.

JIM HACKER: Industrial Harmony?! You know what that means, don't you? That means strikes. From now on every strike in Great Britain will be my fault.

JIM HACKER: I'm not going away. One day you are out of your office, the next day you are out of office.

Asking which member of the Cabinet will be our new PM is like asking which lunatic should run the asylum.

Prime Ministers have little choice in forming governments. There are only 630 MPs and a party with just over 300 MPs forms a government – and of these 300, 100 are too old and silly to be ministers and 100 too young and callow. Therefore there are about 100 MPs to fill 100 government posts. Effectively no choice at all.

I gather he was as drunk as a lord, so after a discreet interval they will probably make him one.

A Prime Minister spends two days appointing the members of his Cabinet and five years disappointing them.

The Prime Minister doesn't think it's silly to appoint people who are vain and incompetent. Look at the Cabinet.

Ministers with a grip on the job are a nuisance because:

a.   They argue
b.   They start to learn the facts
c.   They ask if you have carried out instructions they gave you six months ago
d.   If you tell them something is impossible they may dig out an old submission in which you said it was easy.

Official secrets

He that would keep a secret must keep it secret that he has a secret to keep.

An irregular verb: I give confidential press briefings; you leak; he's being charged under section 2A of the Official Secrets Act.

BERNARD WOOLLEY: But can a £74 million building project on a nine-acre site in the middle of a city be swept under the carpet?

SIR HUMPHREY: We'll use the Official Secrets Act.

BERNARD WOOLLEY: But how can it possibly be a secret? It's so huge.

SIR HUMPHREY: It's a big secret, Bernard.

JIM HACKER: Tiny mistake? £75,000 wasted! Give me an example of a big mistake.

SIR HUMPHREY: Letting people find out about it.

SIR HUMPHREY: How are things at the Campaign for the Freedom of Information, by the way?

SIR ARNOLD: Sorry, I cannot talk about that.

Open government is a contradiction in terms: you can be open or you can have government.

BERNARD WOOLLEY: Shall I file it?
JIM HACKER: File it? Shred it!
BERNARD WOOLLEY: Shred it??
JIM HACKER: Nobody must ever be able to find it again.
BERNARD WOOLLEY: In that case, Minister, I think it is best I file it.

We don't suppress reports. Suppression is the instrument of totalitarian dictatorship; we don't do that sort of thing in a free country. We simply take a democratic decision not to publish it.

It is understood if ministers need to know anything it will be brought to their notice. If they go out looking for information, they might find it.

SIR ARNOLD: Are you suggesting that I give confidential information to the press?
SIR HUMPHREY: Certainly not, Arnold. This is confidential disinformation.
SIR ARNOLD: Ah, that is different.

The Official Secrets Act is not to protect secrets, it is to protect officials.

We are calling the White Paper 'Open Government' because you always dispose of the difficult bit in the title. It does less harm there than on the statute books.

Open Government is rather like the live theatre: in order to have something you are prepared to show openly, there must first be much hidden activity.

Damned lies and statistics

SIR HUMPHREY: Minister, you said you wanted the administration figures reduced, didn't you?

JIM HACKER: Yes.

SIR HUMPHREY: So we reduced the figures.

JIM HACKER: But only the figures, not the number of administrators.

SIR HUMPHREY: Well, of course not.

JIM HACKER: This government believes in reducing bureaucracy.

LUDOVIC KENNEDY: Well, figures that I have here say that your department's staff has risen by 10 per cent.

JIM HACKER: Certainly not.

LUDOVIC KENNEDY: Well, what figure do you have?

JIM HACKER: I believe the figure is much more like 9.97.

SIR HUMPHREY: If local authorities don't send us the statistics that we ask for, then government figures will be a nonsense.

JIM HACKER: Why?

SIR HUMPHREY: They will be incomplete.

JIM HACKER: But government figures are a nonsense anyway.

BERNARD WOOLLEY: I think Sir Humphrey wants to ensure they are a complete nonsense.

Doing the honours

SIR HUMPHREY: There is no reason to change the honours system, which has worked so well in the past.

JIM HACKER: But it hasn't.

SIR HUMPHREY: But. . . we've got to give the present system a fair trial.

JIM HACKER: Ah yes, I thought you might say that. It may interest you to know, Humphrey, that the Most Noble Order of the Garter was founded in 1348 by King Edward III. I think perhaps it may be coming towards the end of its trial period now, don't you?

JIM HACKER: Nice to be able to reward one's old allies. Was Ron Jones pleased with his peerage?

BERNARD WOOLLEY: Oh yes, Prime Minister. He said his members would be delighted.

JIM HACKER: His members?

BERNARD WOOLLEY: Yes, the members of his union. The National Federation—

JIM HACKER: I didn't mean him. I meant our backbencher. I meant to give a peerage to Ron Jones, not Ron Jones. The hell!!

BERNARD WOOLLEY: If it is any consolation, Prime Minister, I gather he was awfully pleased.

JIM HACKER: What are we going to do about Ron Jones's peerage? Give him one too?

SIR HUMPHREY: With respect, Prime Minister, we can't send two Lord Ron Jones to the Upper House. It will look like a job lot.

JIM HACKER: We've got to give him something. I promised.

SIR HUMPHREY: Well, what is he interested in? Does he watch television?

JIM HACKER: He hasn't even got a set.

SIR HUMPHREY: Fine, make him a governor of the BBC.

JIM HACKER: When did a civil servant last refuse an honour?

BERNARD WOOLLEY: Well, I think there was somebody in the Treasury that refused a knighthood.

JIM HACKER: Good God. When?

BERNARD WOOLLEY: I think it was 1496.

JIM HACKER: Why?

BERNARD WOOLLEY: He'd already got one.

Spinning like a top

JIM HACKER: But the broad strategy in reforming local government is to cut ruthlessly at waste while leaving essential services intact.

LUDOVIC KENNEDY: Well, that is what your predecessor said. Are you saying that he failed?

JIM HACKER: Please, let me finish, because we must be absolutely clear about this, and I would be quite frank with you, the plain fact of the matter is that at the end of the day it is the right – no, the duty – of the elected government in the House of Commons to ensure that government policies, the policies on which we were elected and for which we have a mandate, the policies after all for which the people voted, are the policies which finally when the national cake has been divided up, and may I remind you we as a nation don't have unlimited wealth, so we can't pay ourselves more than we've earned, are the policies. . . I'm sorry, what was the question again?

SIR ARNOLD: I presume the Prime Minister is in favour of this scheme because it will reduce unemployment?

SIR HUMPHREY: Well, it looks as if he's reducing unemployment.

SIR ARNOLD: Or looks as if he's trying to reduce unemployment.

SIR HUMPHREY: Whereas in reality he's only trying to look as if he's trying to reduce unemployment.

SIR ARNOLD: Yes, because he's worried that it does not look as if he's trying to look as if he's trying to reduce unemployment.

BERNARD WOOLLEY: Well, thinking back on what I said, and what they said, and what I said you said, and what they may say I said you said, or what they may have thought I said I thought you thought, well, they may say I said I thought you said you thought. . .

JIM HACKER: Go on, Bernard.

BERNARD WOOLLEY: Well, I think I said you said you thought. . . you were above the law.

JIM HACKER: YOU SAID THAT?!

BERNARD WOOLLEY: Well, not intentionally. It is just the way it came out. I am terribly sorry but they were asking me all these questions.

JIM HACKER: Bernard, just because people ask you questions, what makes you think you have to answer them?

BERNARD WOOLLEY: Well, I don't know.

JIM HACKER: You never answer my questions just because I ask them.

You don't want to go on record as saying somebody is no good. You must be seen to be their friend. It is necessary to get behind someone before you can stab them in the back.

SIR HUMPHREY: Well, perhaps you could advise me, Prime Minister. Particularly if the questions are aggressive.

JIM HACKER: Oh, the more aggressive the better. That puts the listeners on your side.

SIR HUMPHREY: Nonetheless, I may have to answer them.

JIM HACKER: Why? You never answered my questions.

SIR HUMPHREY: That's different, Prime Minister.

The fourth estate

In Whitehall and Westminster, information is currency and the lobby correspondents run the principal bureau de change.

....

SIR HUMPHREY: The interview was over. We were just chatting, harmlessly.
BERNARD WOOLLEY: Harmlessly?!
SIR HUMPHREY: It was off-the-record!
BERNARD WOOLLEY: It was on the tape!!

....

It is sometimes difficult to explain to ministers that open government can sometimes mean informing their Cabinet colleagues as well as their friends in Fleet Street.

'Restricted' means it was in the papers yesterday. 'Confidential' means it won't be in the papers until today.

If you believe the security of the realm is at risk you don't hold a security inquiry, you call in the Special Branch. Government security inquiries are only used for killing press stories.

Solved problems aren't news. Tell the press a story in two halves: the problem first and the solution later. Then they get a disaster story one day and a triumph story the next.

We should always tell the press, freely and frankly, anything that they can easily find out some other way.

Speeches are not written for the audience to which they are delivered. Delivering the speech is merely the formality that has to be gone through in order to get the press release into the newspapers.

No communiqué ever bears any relation to what you actually say. It's just a sort of visa. Gets you past the press corps.

Stating the obvious

'Cynic' is the word used by an idealist to describe a realist.

Avoiding precedents does not mean nothing should ever be done. It only means that nothing should ever be done for the first time.

No one really understands the true nature of fawning servility until he sees an academic who has glimpsed the prospect of money or personal publicity.

It is really hard to explain to the public that the waste of £40 million is a small sum of money. But in fact it is tiny compared with the amount wasted on Blue Streak, the TSR2, Trident, Concorde, Nimrod, high-rise council flats, British Rail, British Leyland, Upper Clyde shipbuilders, the atomic power station programme, comprehensive schools or the University of Essex.

JIM HACKER: Yes, well, this is serious.

CHIEF WHIP: Very serious.

SIR HUMPHREY: Very serious.

JIM HACKER: What could happen if either of them became PM?

SIR HUMPHREY: Something very serious indeed.

CHIEF WHIP: Very serious.

JIM HACKER: I see. . .

CHIEF WHIP: Serious repercussions.

SIR HUMPHREY: Serious repercussions.

CHIEF WHIP: Of the utmost seriousness.

JIM HACKER: Yes, that is serious.

SIR HUMPHREY: In fact, I would go so far as to say that it could hardly be more serious.

JIM HACKER: Well, I think we all agree, then: this is serious.

JIM HACKER: As you know, I have got to appoint a new Governor of the Bank of England. I'd welcome your views.

SIR DESMOND: Well, I certainly think you should appoint one.

BERNARD WOOLLEY: This M40 is a very good road.

JIM HACKER: So is the M4. I wonder why we got two really good roads to Oxford, before we got any to Southampton, Dover or Lowestoft or any of the ports?

BERNARD WOOLLEY: Nearly all our Permanent Secretaries went to Oxford, Minister. And most Oxford colleges give very good dinners.

JIM HACKER: And the Cabinet let them get away with it?

BERNARD WOOLLEY: Certainly not, they put their foot down. They said no motorway to take civil servants to dinners in Oxford, unless there was a motorway to take Cabinet ministers hunting in the shires. That's why when the M1 was built in the fifties it stopped in the middle of Leicestershire.

Surveillance is an indispensable weapon in the battle against organised crime. And disorganised crime, like politics.

SIR HUMPHREY: The people are ignorant and misguided.

JIM HACKER: Humphrey, it was the people who elected me.

JIM HACKER: It is not in my interest. And I represent the public, so it is not in the public interest.

All politics is local

JIM HACKER: Half the local councillors you meet are self-centred busybodies on a four-year ego trip, and the other half are in it for what they can get out of it.

SIR HUMPHREY: Perhaps they ought to be in the House of Commons— I mean, to see how a proper legislative assembly behaves.

JIM HACKER: What are you saying?

SIR HUMPHREY: I am saying that education will never get any better as long as it's subject to all that tomfoolery in the town halls. I mean, just imagine what would happen if you put defence in the hands of the local authorities.

JIM HACKER: Defence?

SIR HUMPHREY: Yes, give the local councils a hundred million each and ask them to defend themselves. We wouldn't have to worry about the Russians; we would have a civil war in three weeks.

SIR HUMPHREY: You just don't leave important matters in the hands of local councils. And as you've left education to them, one must assume that until now you've attached little importance to it.

JIM HACKER: I think it is extremely important. It could lose me the next election.

SIR HUMPHREY: Ah!! In my naivety, I thought you were concerned about the future of our children.

JIM HACKER: Yes, that too. They get the vote at eighteen.

Local democracy is a farce. Nobody knows who their local councillors are. Three quarters don't even vote in the local elections and the ones that do just treat it as a popularity poll on the government at Westminster.

Central government must not interfere with the democratic right of freely elected local councils to pour ratepayers' money down the drain.

Asking a town hall to slim down its staff is like asking an alcoholic to blow up a distillery.

State of health

Why should we close a hospital because it has no patients? We don't disband the Army just because there isn't a war.

Moral principles require the government to ban smoking. But when £4 billion pounds of revenue is at stake, we have to consider very seriously how far we are entitled to indulge ourselves in the rather selfish luxury of pursuing moral principles.

The National Health Service is not an advanced case of galloping bureaucracy. It is a gentle canter, at the most.

There is no point in the Cabinet questioning the Treasury. On the rare occasions when the Treasury understands the question, the Cabinet does not understand the answers.

The Treasury was rather more competent before the invention of the Xerox than it is now, because its officials had so much less to read.

JIM HACKER: Bernard, Humphrey should have seen this coming and warned me.

BERNARD WOOLLEY: I don't think Sir Humphrey understands economics, Prime Minister; he did read Classics, you know.

JIM HACKER: What about Sir Frank? He's head of the Treasury!

BERNARD WOOLLEY: Well, I'm afraid he's at an even greater disadvantage in understanding economics: he's an economist.

The Treasury does not work out what it needs and then think how to raise the money. It pitches for as much as it can get away with and then thinks how to spend it.

The art of the possible

Politicians like to panic, they need activity. It's their substitute for achievement.

If we, the right people, don't have power, do you know what happens? The wrong people get it!

Any statement in a politician's memoir can represent one of six different levels of reality:
a.   What happened
b.   What he believed happened
c.   What he would like to have happened
d.   What he wants to believe happened
e.   What he wants other people to believe happened
f.   What he wants other people to believe he believed happened.

The security excuse is the last resort of a desperate politician.

A good political speech is not one in which you can prove that the man is telling the truth; it is one where no one else can prove he is lying.

Almost anything can be attacked as a failure, but almost anything can be defended as not a significant failure. Politicians do not appreciate the significance of 'significant'.

A politician's dilemma: He must obviously follow his conscience, but he must also know where he's going. So he can't follow his conscience, because it may not be going the same way that he is.

Politics as defined by *Roget's Thesaurus*: Manipulation, Intrigue, Wire-Pulling, Evasion, Rabble-Rousing, Graft.

Politician's logic:
1. We must do something
2. This is something
3. Therefore we must do this.

[Sir Humphrey claims he would be deeply sorry to see the minister leave the DAA.]

JIM HACKER: Yes, I suppose we have got rather fond of one another. In a way.

SIR HUMPHREY: *[laughs]* In a way, yes!

JIM HACKER: *[jokingly]* Like a terrorist and his hostage!

BERNARD WOOLLEY: Which one of you is the terrorist?

HACKER AND SIR HUMPHREY: *[each points at the other]* He is.

Ministers decide

Basic ministerial skills:
1. Blurring issues
2. Delaying decisions
3. Dodging questions
4. Juggling figures
5. Bending facts
6. Concealing errors.

Ministers, unlike civil servants, are selected completely at random by prime ministerial whim, in recognition of doubtful favours received, or to avoid appointing someone of real ability who might become a threat.

There are two types of chair for two types of minister. Those that fold up instantly and those that just go round in circles.

There are a number of issues about which a minister automatically tells lies, and he would be regarded as foolish or incompetent if he told the truth.

To a minister the word 'courageous' is even worse than 'controversial'. 'Controversial' only means it will lose you votes; 'courageous' means it will lose you the election.

Presenting proposals to ministers:

1. Ministers will generally accept proposals which contain the words 'simple', 'quick', 'popular' and 'cheap'.
2. Ministers will generally throw out proposals which contain the words 'complicated', 'lengthy', 'expensive' and 'controversial'.
3. If you wish to describe a proposal in a way that guarantees that a minister will reject it, describe it as courageous.

Civil servants do not see it as part of their job to help ministers make fools of themselves. They have never met one who needed any help.

Ministers can never go anywhere without their briefs, in case they get caught with their trousers down.

If you are not happy with a minister's decision there is no need to argue him out of it. Accept it warmly, and then suggest he leaves it to you to work out the details.

A decision is a decision only if it is the decision you wanted. Otherwise, it is merely the course the minister seems to favour at the moment.

Ministers do not believe they exist unless they are reading about themselves in the newspapers.

The pact the Civil Service offers to ministers: If the minister will help us implement the opposite policy to the one to which he is pledged, we will help him pretend that he is in fact doing what he said he was going to do.

A minister's absence is the best cover for not informing him of things it is better he should not know. And, for the next six months, if he complains of not having been informed about something, you can tell him it came up while he was away.

To watch a Cabinet minister in action is to watch the endless subordination of long-term important issues to the demands of urgent trivia.

Ministers are always vulnerable when they are in a hurry. That is why we always keep them busy.

SIR HUMPHREY: Bernard, ministers should never know more than they need to know. Then they can't tell anyone. Like secret agents, they could be captured and tortured.
BERNARD WOOLLEY: You mean by terrorists?
SIR HUMPHREY: By the BBC, Bernard.

It is not necessarily necessary to let ministers know what everybody else knows.

Functions of a minister:

1. He is an advocate. He makes the department's actions seem plausible to Parliament and the public.
2. He is our man in Westminster, steering our legislation through Parliament (NB: ours, not his).
3. He is our breadwinner. His duty is to fight in Cabinet for the money we need to do our job.

Every new minister we have had would have been a laughing stock within his first three weeks in office if it had not been for the most rigid and impenetrable secrecy about what he was up to.

The Industry Secretary is the idlest man in town, the Education Secretary's the most illiterate and the Employment Secretary unemployable.

If a minister is allowed to run his department, the results are:

1. Chaos
2. Innovations
3. Public debate
4. Outside scrutiny.

Ministers are not experts. Ministers are put in charge precisely because they know nothing.

Ministers moving to the House of Lords receive approbation, elevation and castration, all in one stroke.

Sir Humphrey: So we trust you to make sure that your minister does nothing incisive or divisive over the next few weeks.

Sir Arnold: Avoids anything controversial.

Sir Humphrey: Expresses no firm opinion about anything at all. Now, is that quite clear?

Bernard Woolley: Yes, well, I think that is probably what he was planning to do anyway.

We do not mind whether the minister is re-elected or not. As far as this department is concerned, it makes very little difference who the minister is.

Benefits of Ministerial Absence: A minister's absence is desirable because it enables you to do the job properly. There will be no:

1.   silly questions
2.   bright ideas
3.   fussing about what the papers are saying.

Of the people, for the people

Basic rules of government:
1. Never look into anything you don't have to.
2. Never set up an inquiry unless you know in advance what its findings will be.
3. Never hold a meeting until you have written the minutes.
4. Never begin a conference until you have agreed the final communiqué.
5. Always write the conclusion before you look for the evidence.

The useful life of a government is about eighteen months. The first year is taken up with discovering that they can't do what they promised in their manifesto. The second year is spent finding out what they can do. Then there are eighteen months of useful work. After that the next election is too close, so there follow eighteen months of pre-election paralysis.

Government is about principles. And the principle is, never act on principle.

Government is not about morality, it is about stability, keeping things going, preventing anarchy, stopping society falling to bits. Still being here tomorrow.

Turning a blind eye to corruption could never be government policy. It is merely government practice.

A week may be a long time in politics but a year is a short time in government.

All government departments are lobbies for the pressure groups they deal with. The Department of Health lobbies for the doctors and hospital unions, the Department of Energy lobbies for the oil companies and so on. So each department of state is actually controlled by the people it is supposed to be controlling.

There has to be a nuclear bunker in Whitehall. Government doesn't stop merely because the country has been destroyed. Annihilation is bad enough, without anarchy to make it worse.

The government is not a team, it's a loose confederation of warring tribes.

Government is about principle. And the principle is: don't rock the boat. Because if you do rock the boat all the little consciences fall out.

You do not open a national debate until the government has privately made up its mind.

Government isn't about good and evil; it's only about order and chaos.

Most government departments achieve the opposite of their purpose: the Commonwealth Office lost us the Commonwealth, the Department of Industry reduced industry, the Department of Transport presided over the disintegration of our public transport system and the Treasury loses our money.

Government security enquiries are only for killing press stories. Their sole purpose is to enable the Prime Minister to stand up in the House and say we have held a full enquiry and there is no evidence to substantiate these charges.

It's no good saying something is common sense. Government policy has nothing to do with common sense.

Practically everything that happens in government is suspicious.

Official drivers are one of the most useful sources of information in Whitehall. Passengers forget that everything they say in the back seat can be overheard in the front.

It's well known that social problems increase to occupy the total number of social workers available to deal with them.

Rules of the game

The three most unreliable things in public life are political memoirs, official denials and manifesto promises.

A career in politics is no preparation for government.

Facts complicate things. All that the press, the people and their elected leaders want to know is who are the goodies and who are the baddies.

Gratitude is merely a lively expectation of favours to come.

If a job's worth doing, it's worth delegating.

When anybody says 'It's not the money, it's the principle' they mean 'It's the money'.

The first rule of politics: Never believe anything until it's been officially denied.

Diplomacy is about surviving till the next century. Politics is about surviving till Friday afternoon.

Elevation from the House of Commons to the House of Lords is like being moved from the animals to the vegetables.

The hypothetical example is an excellent way of deflecting attention from real problems.

No, Prime Minister

Review of *Yes Prime Minister* by Jim Hacker
Sir Humphrey Appleby (PUNCH, December 3, 1986)

When I entered the civil service in the 1950s it was still possible
for a man of intelligence and ingenuity to defend the thesis that
politics was an honourable profession. Ministers did not divulge
Cabinet proceedings. Leaking to the press was regarded as a
breach of confidence, not as an instrument of government. And
if a department fell down badly on a job, the minister resigned.
Equally, members of the Civil Service preserved a cloak of
anonymity and a tradition of discreet silence which concealed
from the rest of the country the fact that they were running it.

I state this as a preface since it may otherwise be hard to
communicate to the reader the reasons why *Yes Prime Minister:
The Diaries of the Rt Hon James Hacker MP* is so reprehensible
a work (if the word 'work' may appropriately be used in
connection with its author). The uninstructed may gain
pleasure, and believe they are being vouchsafed privileged
insights, by reading these distressingly frank accounts of how the
author reached his main political decisions (or, more frequently,
indecisions). The style has certain liveliness, often achieved by
those without the reflective profundity to appreciate, or the
intellectual apparatus to communicate, those qualifications and
modifications which may make the account less readable but
which do render it reliable. As a result, the seeker after truth, if
he is unwise enough to pick up this book at all, must be aware
that any statement of Mr Hacker's may describe:

a) what happened
b) what he believed happened
c) what he would like to believe happened
d) what he wanted others to believe happened
e) what he wanted others to believe he believed happened.

Taken at this level, the book may be regarded as entertaining gossip, but should not be used as source material and indeed would be better treated as fiction than history.

More important, however, than the book itself is the fact that revelations of this sort should ever be published at all. The old tradition of the responsible minister and his obedient servant is apparently transformed into a totally misleading portrait of scheming officials manipulating innocent politicians. Although those at the heart of government are aware that this is an absurd travesty, there is a danger that simple-minded souls may be deceived into believing there may be some truth in it.

Perhaps Hacker is not to blame. The rot began with the Crossman Diaries: and once one minister reveals the secrets of the Cabinet, the others rush in to 'set the record straight', which of course means so to distort events as to show themselves in favourable light. After reading a succession of descriptions of the same period from opposed ministers, all of whom were by their own account uniformly honourable in their dealings and right in their judgments, it is hard to see where to lay the responsibility for decades of unprecedented and unrelieved political squalor.

The only scapegoat available must therefore logically be the Civil Service. This has culminated in a distressing and regrettable change in public opinion, so that the necessary role of the civil service in advising caution, taking soundings, consulting

colleagues, examining precedents, preparing options, and
advising ministers on the likely consequences of their proposals
if they reached the statute books, is perceived as ingrained
bureaucratic obstructiveness rather than an attempt to translate
narrow political expediency into broad national benefit.

I realise that in criticising the Hacker diaries from this
standpoint one may be laying oneself open to a charge of
defending the narrow interests of the Civil Service against
the great benefits of more openness about government.
Paradoxically, this has not been the case. When I first attended
Cabinet as a Private Secretary in the 1960s, members were
irritated by the stultifying boredom of the proceedings and
would interrupt with diverting outbursts of truth which
would cause much conflict and dissent. When I returned to
Cabinet in the 1980s, they were all peacefully occupied making
notes for their memoirs and would make only the statements
they wanted the others to record in theirs. This has been
enormously beneficial to the Civil Service, for an interesting
reason: the fact is that the movement to 'open up' government,
if successful, always achieves a gratifying increase in level of
security. The reason is obvious. Once a meeting – Parliament,
local council, Cabinet – is opened up to the public, it is used by
those attending as a propaganda platform and not as a genuine
debating forum. The true discussions take place privately in
smaller informal groups. In government these smaller groups
often contain one or more senior civil servants, so that some
element of intelligence and practicability can be built into
proposals before they become public and have to be defended
with arguments which represent a victory of personal pride
over common sense. So the move to greater openness in public
affairs has greatly strengthened the level of secrecy and therefore

the quality of decision-making in the higher echelons of government.

I started out on a somewhat gloomy note about the decline in the quality of government over the period in which I have been privileged to serve in. Perhaps I should end on a more genial reflection. This period of decline in political standards and national standing has been matched (though obviously not caused) by a gratifying growth in the size and influence of the Civil Service. Many of its members might reflect that the title 'Paradise Postponed' does not reflect the post-war period as they have observed it. 'Paradise Achieved' would be more apt. It has seen a tremendous growth in the peacetime Civil Service as compared with the pre-war period, a vast surge in public expenditure, the welcome adjustment of salary levels in the top echelons of the service to render them broadly comparable with similar rewards in banking and oil, the indexation of pensions and the continuation of honours for service. Since Mr Hacker was in the Cabinet for an important part of this period, we can perhaps forgive him those lapses in discretion and accuracy that mar his book in recompense for the greater good his period of office achieved, even if only by accident.

Like Yes Prime Minister *itself, this book review is by Jonathan Lynn and Antony Jay.*

Obituaries

Sir Bernard Woolley KCB
Born 15 July 1944, died 4 November 1995

Despite his first in Greats, few of Bernard Woolley's contemporaries would have expected him to end his career as Cabinet Secretary and head of the Civil Service. He was a genial and easy-going colleague, but did not – at least in his early appointments – show any sign that he was cut out for leadership, and his first private secretaryship was to the comparatively lowly Department of Administrative Affairs. It was, however, to prove a formative experience. His minister was Jim Hacker, a politician who had never previously held government office, and whose interests, it has to be said, were more in securing personal and political advantage than in the impartial and orderly conduct of the nation's affairs. This created for Woolley a conflict between his natural instinct to avoid confrontation and his obligation to uphold, and to impress on his minister, the standards of conduct and rules of procedure that the Civil Service expected of Cabinet ministers.

In this he had two advantages.

The first was that Hacker, while not lacking a certain political guile, was ignorant of the machinery of government after a parliamentary career spent entirely in opposition, and furthermore had neither the intellect nor the willpower to conduct an effective campaign against the system. The second advantage was that his Permanent Secretary was Sir Humphrey Appleby, a true mandarin of the old school, who supplied the backbone that nature had denied to Woolley. Appleby was a devout believer in keeping ministers in their place, leaving it to the experts in the Civil Service to conduct the nation's affairs in a consistent and disciplined manner. This underlying conflict between the aims of his ministers and those of his Permanent Secretary could have made life difficult for a new Private Secretary, but in fact it proved to be the making of Woolley. His charm, his helpfulness and his essentially amenable nature gained his minister's confidence, while his loyalty to the service and his commitment to its standards kept Sir Humphrey reasonably satisfied with his discharge of a Private Secretary's duties. It was indeed no small achievement to keep the peace between two men whose personalities and objectives were so widely at variance, and Woolley must be given full credit for it.

It is clear in retrospect that this was the high point in Woolley's professional career. The decline began with the wholly unexpected elevation of Jim Hacker to the premiership. Against Sir Humphrey's advice Hacker took Woolley with him into Downing Street as Private Secretary to the Prime Minister, raising him to a level of seniority he could never have expected, and no one would have forecast, when he entered the service. For a while he continued to fulfil his useful function as a buffer between Hacker and Appleby, but after Hacker's resignation he was promoted to Permanent Secretary and then, with the election of a new government and Sir Humphrey's retirement, to Cabinet Secretary. It was then that the qualities of emollient diplomacy and discreet compromise, which had served him so well in the more junior role, proved to be his undoing when something more robust was called for.

The new government arrived with a commitment to informality and a determination to impose its party political will on the civil service communications machine. Decisions which used to be taken round the table in the Cabinet Room at Number 10 were now taken on the sofa in the study, and political advisors who had previously been politely sidelined by officials were now given formal authority over them. Such innovations would have appalled Sir Humphrey, who could have been trusted to resist them *à l'outrance*, but Woolley did not have the subtlety or the steel of his predecessor. Some of his colleagues urged him to refuse to implement the new system and challenge the Prime Minister to dismiss him. Others believed he should resign, making his reasons public. In the end, however, his predilection for co-operation and compromise, and his distaste for confrontation, overcame his personal instincts and his professional principles, and in the words of a contemporary political commentator, 'like an inverted Julius Caesar, he came, he saw and he concurred'.

With the benefit of hindsight we can see the disastrous consequences of both of Bernard Woolley's capitulations. Informal decision-making led to unparalleled confusion and inefficiency in the higher reaches of government, and giving political advisors formal authority over career civil servants steadily turned government information into party propaganda. Many political historians attribute to these two decisions the subsequent public contempt for politicians, political institutions and also political processes which reached its apogee with the parliamentary expenses scandal many

years later in the spring of 2009. It would be unjust to hold Woolley exclusively accountable for all the weaknesses and failures that characterised the years subsequent to his appointment, and it is by no means certain that a courageous and principled stand on his part would in fact have served to protect the formalities and proprieties of the Appleby era from the depredations of the incoming modernisers. Woolley himself always maintains that the change was inevitable, and that he could be of more use staying in his place and working to mitigate its worst effects than departing in a dramatic gesture which left others to clean up the mess. Clearly we shall never know, but equally clearly the Bernard Woolley years will never be remembered amongst the most glorious in the history of Her Majesty's Civil Service.

While he did not have that many admirers, his warm personality and inexhaustible good nature ensured that he had a large number of friends, and he was always a popular figure at the public events he attended regularly, and in the charitable organisations to which he generously gave so much of his time after his retirement. His favourite activity was his work as advisory editor to the *Oxford Dictionary of Quotations*, and he is remembered with respect and affection at Oxford University Press.

Lord Hacker of Islington, KG, Hon. DPhil
Born 18 June 1927, died 4 November 1995

James (Jim) Hacker was perhaps not the most naturally gifted of Britain's Prime Ministers, but few even of his opponents denied the force of his personal charm or his sense of what the voting public wanted. Like many of his contemporaries in the party, a long period in opposition had sharpened his appetite for power without perhaps providing him with the necessary training for exercising it effectively.

His appointment as Minister for Administrative Affairs was no more than he could have expected as a reward for his loyal support for his leader in opposition, and he took up the reins of office with a number of excellent intentions. His policy initiatives showed his sensitivity to popular feeling, and indeed he was in some ways a pioneer of reforms which were implemented by others long after he had left office.

He was an early advocate of open government, of national health reform and of an integrated transport system, and his political memoirs also show his interest in other still active issues such as cutting government waste and increasing representation of women in the higher ranks of the Civil Service.

It is still something of a mystery why none of these ever reached the statute book during his tenure in office. His critics have attributed this to his inability or reluctance to think measures through and examine their implications before announcing them. Others attribute this failure to spending too long on the opposition front bench, where success is measured by an ability to formulate attractive-sounding ideas and encapsulate them in catchy phrases (at which he was expert) without ever having to draft legislation and take it through Parliament. It is certainly true that his professional career in political research, university lecturing and journalism had never required him to engage with the relatively tedious and unglamorous task of motivating staff, controlling budgets or running even the smallest of departments, nor with the acceptance of managerial responsibility for anything.

But this was true of many of his Cabinet colleagues, who nevertheless produced solid and successful legislation. What makes this especially surprising is that throughout his spell at the department he had as his Permanent Secretary the legendary Sir Humphrey

Appleby, one of the safest pairs of hands in the history of the Civil Service. Moreover, his Private Secretary was the brilliant young high flyer Bernard Woolley, later to become Cabinet Secretary himself. With such an expert team behind him, Hacker's inability to register any significant legislative achievement (except for small liberalisation of data protection rules) can certainly not be attributed to any lack of firmness or skill in his administrative support.

Hacker's career took a dramatic change of direction after two years at the Department of Administrative Affairs. The Prime Minister suddenly resigned, for reasons which have never been adequately explained. It was a particularly startling resignation, since his natural successor, the Home Secretary, had only two days previously had to resign over a drunken driving incident on the way home after recording a Christmas 'Don't drink and drive' broadcast. As party chairman, Hacker had an important role in organising the succession, which was assumed to lie between the Chancellor of the Exchequer and the Foreign Secretary. It is still not fully understood why both of them decided to withdraw from the contest; even Hacker's most fervent supporters do not suggest it was because they both recognised his superior strength of character and intellectual abilities.

Nevertheless, their bitter rivalry made their withdrawal a great relief to the party, and started a search for a less divisive leader. Even so, it was a considerable surprise even to the closest political observers when Hacker's name finally went forward unopposed.

Not the least of Hacker's pleasures on entering Number 10 must have been his reunion with his old Permanent Secretary, Sir Humphrey Appleby. Sir Humphrey had been appointed Cabinet Secretary only a few days before the resignation of the Prime Minister and was waiting there to welcome his successor. Since Hacker brought with him Bernard Woolley, his departmental Private Secretary, the old team was now reunited at an eminence they can scarcely have foreseen when they first met on the steps of the Department of Administrative Affairs that Monday morning after the general election.

A change of Prime Minister always provokes expectations of a renaissance or a reformation, and Hacker was anxious to make his mark on events as early as possible. He selected defence as an area where radical reorganisation could produce spectacular savings and an improvement in efficiency at the same time. His proposal to sell off most of the expensive defence and real estate in north London and south-east England and relocate their staff to high-unemployment areas in the north could indeed have had considerable economic impact – and political impact too, since many of the designated high-unemployment areas turned out to be in marginal constituencies. Unfortunately, the senior officers in the armed forces were able to demonstrate that although they strongly approved of the policy, it would not in fact be practicable in their particular establishments. The unspoken objection that it would put their wives out of shopping range from Harrods and Harvey Nichols was, of course no more than a light-hearted political canard.

In the same way, his proposal to cancel a major part of Britain's nuclear weapons programme and use the money to reintroduce National Service was welcomed by many people outside the defence establishment. But here too the general staff were able to demonstrate that his scheme, while eminently commendable in theory, could not be made to work in practice. After this, Hacker appeared to run out of steam, and the rest of his premiership was spent largely in responding to events rather than seizing them and shaping them. The reformer in him had a brief revival when he investigated the possibility of abolishing the Department of Education. But although the proposals were judged by many educational experts to be both imaginative and feasible, they followed his other proposed reforms into the sand. The subsequent election defeat, though seen by his party as a tragedy, can with hindsight be judged, at least in his case, as a merciful release.

Hacker's premiership will not go down in history as a spectacular success or a dismal failure. Most probably it will be relegated to that brief chapter occupied by Rosebery, Bonar Law, Douglas Home and Callaghan: too brief to be memorable and characterised, if at all, by what occurred during it rather than by what it achieved. This is perhaps a pity, even an injustice. Hacker was a decent, likeable man, with some commendable reforming intentions. He had the misfortune of not being able to impose his schemes on those who would have to implement them, despite the sterling support of powerful officials like Sir Humphrey Appleby and Bernard Woolley. He was always open to advice and ideas, but seemed puzzled, if not paralysed, when they conflicted. In his favour it can be said that he provided a focus for unity in the party at the time when it was sorely needed; his weakness was that he saw his chief and, as time went on, his only duty as being to secure his re-election. When he failed in this there was little if anything to mark his tenure of a premiership which, if the truth be told, brought more distinction to him than he brought to the office which he briefly occupied.

Sir Humphrey Appleby
Born 5 April 1929, died 4 November 1995

Sir Humphrey Appleby was perhaps the most outstanding civil servant of this generation. The principles he formulated, the practices he instituted and the probity he exemplified have become the model for his successors right up to the present day.

After a classical scholarship to Winchester, and a first in Greats at Balliol College, Oxford, followed by two years' National Service in the Army Education Corps, he entered the Civil Service as an assistant principal in the Scottish Office. His administrative gifts were soon recognised, and when the Department of Administrative Affairs was set up in 1964, he was brought into it as Assistant Secretary. He quickly established himself as a sound official with a safe pair of hands and rose inexorably to the top, becoming Permanent Secretary at a surprisingly young age – in fact he was not yet fifty. The Civil Service is often compared to salad dressing, on the grounds that in both of them the oil rises to the top and the vinegar stays at the bottom, but while Sir Humphrey was certainly not vinegary it would be unjust to ascribe his smooth manner to oiliness. He was indeed in all respects a model of deferential propriety in his dealings with politicians, but underneath his suave and diplomatic exterior there was a firmness of will and clarity of purpose that many ministers came to value.

His qualities were perhaps seen at their best when James Hacker arrived as minister after many years on the opposition benches. The political skills Hacker had developed there, were not, one might say, wholly adequate for the task of running a department of some 20,000 people, with the result that his dependence on the support of his permanent officials was very nearly total. Fortunately Sir Humphrey was more than up to the task of steering him through the ministerial minefields. All he asked in return was freedom to run the department in his own way, without the distractions of political interference.

Recently released documents have shown that in the early days, Hacker did try to persuade him to implement some of the government's manifesto commitments, but Sir Humphrey was always able to demonstrate that they were inconsistent with the orderly and organised administration of government affairs for which he was so justly renowned throughout Whitehall. He was sometimes characterised as a traditionalist of the old school, and even blamed for Britain's failure to adapt to the second half of the twentieth century. It would be fairer to say that he was acutely aware of the dangers of tinkering with an engine that was running smoothly, even if the vehicle it drove was not at the moment winning the race. He was privately scornful of the endless new initiatives proposed by ministers and although change did take place while he was at his post, he cannot be accused of conniving in it in any way.

When the post of Cabinet Secretary fell vacant on Sir Arnold Robinson's retirement, his appointment to it came as no surprise to anyone. No other candidate came within miles of him. What did come as a surprise, however, was the arrival of Hacker in 10 Downing Street only a few weeks later. As a complete outsider in the premiership stakes, he had received no sort of preparation or grooming for his new role, nor for the complex issues of defence, security and foreign affairs that had been well beyond the remit of his previous ministerial portfolio. Once again, a heavy responsibility fell upon Sir Humphrey's shoulders, and once again they proved more than adequate for the burden.

Critics of Hacker's administration have complained that almost nothing was actually achieved during his comparatively brief tenure of office. Others have pointed out that at least there were no disasters. For this latter fact, the credit must go to Sir Humphrey. Hacker frequently lamented that the delays at Number 10 seemed interminable, but his Cabinet Secretary knew that speed was the enemy of good administration. He had in his career spent too many hours cleaning up after snap decisions and panic legislation to be willing to short-circuit established procedures and traditional practices. He was wonderfully meticulous in consulting every interested party about any new proposals, and also about circulating not only the revisions but the revisions of the revisions for further comment. One of his favourite quotations was Bacon's 'Counsels to which Time hath not been called, Time will not ratify'. He also used to say that, in legislation as in medicine, diarrhoea was a much more offensive and dangerous condition than constipation. He showed a commendable caution in his approach to innovation, having found time and time again that words like 'novel', 'bold' and 'imaginative' were heralds of disaster outside the world of literature and the arts (and often there as well). He believed in precedent, in the tried and tested, and in the wisdom of the ages rather than the fashionable idea of the moment.

His minutes, papers and memoranda (many of which are still treasured to this day by their recipients) were models of literary eloquence. He eschewed the temptations of easy brevity and deceptive simplicity, giving every subject extensive evaluation and applying the fullest possible consideration to every contributing fact and conflicting argument. If he were accused of leaving the reader unsure of what conclusion he had finally reached, he would reply that if they wanted the cheap certainties of tabloid journalism, they could go and read *The Sun* or the *News of the World*. His retirement not only deprived the nation of one of its most distinguished public servants; it also marked the end of an era. His successors lacked his skill and determination in resisting pressure for change, and the new breed of politicians were distressingly assertive. To him the steady improvement in Britain's economic performance and standing in the world which followed his departure was a small recompense for the diminution of power and influence of the institution he had so loyally and industriously served for all of his career. He was especially pained by the reduction in size of the Civil Service; he knew that good administration could not be had on the cheap and took pride

in the steady increase in the number of civil servants over the years
when he was head of the Civil Service.

It would be unfair to say that he despised politicians, though
there were none he spoke of with reverence and few with respect.
He believed their role to be important in its way, even if subservient
to his own. He recognised his inability to whip up popular support
for the government's policies, and to defend them to the press
and Parliament, and was happy to leave that job to them. He also
accepted that they were necessary to extract from the Treasury the
budget that good government demanded. His wrath was reserved
for those who tried to use their temporary eminence to change the
practices that had served the country so well for so many centuries.
He was not implacably opposed to reform; he saw some good in
Thomas Cromwell's changes under Henry VIII and he did not
condemn out of hand the Northcote–Trevelyan reforms of 1854,
though he believed it to be too early to pass a final judgement on
them. But he had no time for what he saw as the half-baked ideas
of jumped-up polytechnic lecturers who had never even run a
whelk stall, owing to lack of necessary qualifications. This is not to
say he was undemocratic, though his idea of democracy was not so
much executing the will of the people as securing their consent to
the policies advocated by those qualified to decide on their behalf.

It is unfortunate that he has left no diaries or memoirs, though
not surprising since his discretion was legendary. The less respectful
of his younger colleagues used to say that he would not tell you
the time until he had checked the level of your security clearance.
Perhaps he now appears a figure from a bygone age. The days may
have passed when public men were admired most for their loyalty,
discretion, integrity and ability to quote Plato, but we are not
necessarily the richer for their passing.

MINISTRY OF
ADMINISTRATIVE AFFAIRS

CAST

Rt Hon James Hacker MP Secretary of State for Administrative Affairs, then Prime Minister	Paul Eddington
Sir Humphrey Appleby Permanent Secretary at the Department of Administrative Affairs, then Cabinet Secretary	Nigel Hawthorne
Bernard Woolley Principal Private Secretary	Derek Fowlds
Annie Hacker Jim's wife	Diana Hoddinott
Sir Arnold Robinson Cabinet Secretary	John Nettleton
Frank Weisel Jim's political advisor	Neil Fitzwilliam
Dorothy Wainwright Jim's Number 10 political advisor	Deborah Norton

PRODUCTION TEAM

Antony Jay	Writer
Jonathan Lynn	Writer
Peter Whitmore	Director & producer
Sydney Lotterby	Producer
Ronnie Hazlehurst	Theme tune & series music
Gerald Scarfe	Title cartoons

EPISODES

Yes Minister series 1 (1980)

1. 'Open Government', 25 February
   Newly appointed government minister James Hacker pledges to fight for open government. Now he's come face to face with his chief obstacle - his staff.

2. 'The Official Visit', 3 March
   Hacker seeks political capital in officially welcoming the new leader of an African nation. Instead the visit may prompt Hacker's own exit from political life.

3. 'The Economy Drive', 10 March
   The minister's department is slated for closure. If he and Sir Humphrey want to save it, they'll have to do the unthinkable - work together.

4. 'Big Brother', 17 March
   How to protect citizens' privacy while developing a computer database? The dilemma leads Hacker and Sir Humphrey into a digital duel.

5. 'The Writing on the Wall', 24 March
   The minister's push to slim down the Civil
   Service is too successful. Now his own
   department is scheduled for closure. Can a PR
   campaign for red tape help?

6. 'The Right to Know', 31 March
   An endangered badger colony threatens to
   provoke an environmental protest that could
   prove most embarrassing to Hacker. His
   daughter plans to lead it. In the nude.

7. 'Jobs for the Boys', 7 April
   The minister is proud of his pet government/
   private sector construction partnership. Why
   is Sir Humphrey so adamant about keeping it
   under wraps?

Yes Minister series 2 (1981)

1. 'The Compassionate Society', 23 February
   A brand new hospital with full staff runs
   as an efficient operation. So why is the
   minister obsessed that it has no patients?

2. 'Doing the Honours', 2 March
   Jim's plan to withhold honours unless budget
   cuts are made seems irresistible. But he has
   not counted on Humphrey's old-boy network.

3. 'The Death List', 9 March
   An old petition against electronic
   surveillance comes back to bug Jim, just when
   he discovers a terrorist group has him as an
   assassination target.

4. 'The Greasy Pole'. 16 March
   Plans for a new chemical factory hinge on the
   outcome of an independent report. But
   Jim discovers that even science can be
   manipulated.

5. 'The Devil You Know', 23 March
   A Cabinet reshuffle coincides with an
   appointment in Brussels. Surely Hacker's job
   is safe, after all, he's done all right -
   hasn't he?

6. 'The Quality of Life', 30 March
   A city farm Hacker has vowed to keep open is
   being turned into a car park. How come Sir
   Humphrey is so smug about the whole affair?

7. 'A Question of Loyalty', 6 April
   In a major speech Hacker has declared war on
   government waste. Then a select committee tests
   the minister's loyalty to his department.

Yes Minister series 3 (1982)

1. 'Equal Opportunities', 11 November
   Sir Humphrey doesn't see eye to eye with the
   minister's plan for sexual equality.

2. 'The Challenge', 18 November
   Hacker starts a crusade to make local
   authorities responsible for their
   expenditure. If it wasn't for fallout
   shelters and Ludovic Kennedy...

3. 'The Skeleton in the Cupboard', 25 November
   The 30-year rule is about to reveal the

name of the young civil servant who made a complete mess of a defence contract. For some reason Sir Humphrey seems nervous...

4. 'The Moral Dimension', 2 December
   After signing a huge export order in Qumran, Jim discovers it was obtained through bribery. Does he know the moral dimension of this?

5. 'The Bed of Nails', 9 December
   Jim is asked to formulate an integrated transport policy. But the title of Transport Supremo turns out not to be worth having.

6. 'The Whisky Priest', 16 December
   Jim learns of the fact that British bombs are in the hands of Italian terrorists. But how to bring this grave news to the PM?

7. 'The Middle-class Rip-off', 23 December
   Subsidising a local football club will bring Hacker enormous popularity. Sir Humphrey, however, seems to think subsidy is only for art...

Christmas special (1984)

'Party Games', 17 December
This landmark episode marked the end of the Yes Minister series and paved the way for its sequel, Yes Prime Minister.

The seasonal festivities at the Department of Administrative Affairs are overshadowed by rumours of a Cabinet reshuffle as the Prime

Minister announces that he intends to step down.
The two leading contenders hoping to succeed
him are also persuaded to step down when it's
revealed that civil servants plan to leak details
of past indiscretions. Jim Hacker becomes the
surprise favourite to get the job when the Civil
Service decides to back him.

Yes Prime Minister series 1 (1986)

1. 'The Grand Design', 9 January
   As Prime Minister, Jim's finger is on the
   nuclear button. Confused over some tough
   questions, he comes up with a surprising
   Grand Design for defence...

2. 'The Ministerial Broadcast', 16 January
   As Jim is coached and groomed for a
   television speech of his new defence policy,
   Sir Humphrey is more concerned with what he
   says than how he says it.

3. 'The Smoke Screen', 23 January
   When Jim decides to champion his Health
   Minister's plan to abolish smoking by
   excessive taxation, a horrified Sir Humphrey
   calls in the tobacco lobby to prevent it.

4. 'The Key', 30 January
   A territorial battle between Sir Humphrey
   and Dorothy Wainwright, the PM's political
   advisor, reminds Jim that his Cabinet
   Secretary may have too much power. But Sir
   Humphrey is not about to have his wings
   clipped...

5. 'A Real Partnership', 6 February
   A governmental financial crisis collides
   with plans for a Civil Service pay rise. Sir
   Humphrey has to summon all his skills to get
   past a well-informed PM.

6. 'A Victory for Democracy', 13 February
   Is the Foreign Office carrying out government
   policy or is the government there to carry
   out Foreign Office policy? Hacker is about to
   find out...

7. 'The Bishop's Gambit', 20 February
   When a British nurse is given ten years and
   forty lashes in Qumran, the PM has to decide
   whether to be heartless or mindless. He also
   has to appoint a bishop, a none-too-easy
   choice.

8. 'One of Us', 27 February
   While a sheepdog trapped on an artillery
   range is stealing the PM's headlines, MI5 is
   dropping a bombshell. Its recently deceased
   head turns out to be a Russian spy - worse
   still, Sir Humphrey headed the committee of
   enquiry...

Yes Prime Minister series 2 (1987-8)

1. 'Man Overboard', 3 December
   The Ministry of Defence is in turmoil over
   the Employment Secretary's plan to create
   civilian jobs by moving servicemen north.
   The PM is in favour, until Sir Humphrey hints
   that the Employment Secretary is plotting
   against him...

2. 'Official Secrets', 10 December
   The former PM's memoirs have to be
   scrutinised for security reasons. When Jim
   receives a chapter that makes him look bad,
   it's leaked to the press that he tried to
   suppress its publication.

3. 'A Diplomatic Incident', 17 December
   The sudden death of the former PM, and his
   memoirs, gives Hacker an opportunity to host
   a state occasion... and to make sure his
   predecessor is dead.

4. 'A Conflict of Interest', 31 December
   With the party conference coming up, rumours
   of a scandal in the City do nothing to improve
   the PM's press. Sir Humphrey knows that the
   only way to avoid disaster depends on the
   new Governor of the Bank of England. Can he
   persuade the PM to appoint the right man?

5. 'Power to the People', 7 January
   Hacker is having problems with local
   government. Especially with Agnes Moorhouse
   of Houndsworth Council, who wants to abolish
   parliament, the courts and the monarchy. She
   must be stopped! This calls for Hacker's
   Reform Bill.

6. 'The Patron of the Arts', 14 January
   The PM is planned to speak at the British
   Theatre Awards Dinner, televised to 12
   million viewers. Unfortunately, the Arts
   Council grant has turned out to be less than
   generous... and the director of the National
   Theatre is introducing Hacker's speech.

7. 'The National Education Service', 21 January
   The education system is a disaster. It's time
   for Jim to get a grip on it. He could always
   axe the Department of Education. But what
   would Humphrey say?

8. 'The Tangled Web', 28 January
   Hacker has committed the ultimate political
   sin - lying to the House. Humphrey feels he
   has a moral responsibility to tell the truth
   ... unless Hacker can employ some gentle
   persuasion.